Successful Parenting
A Common-Sense Guide
To Raising Your Teenagers

John S. Leite, Ph.D.
&
J. Kip Parrish, Ph.D.

Health Communications, Inc.
Deerfield Beach, Florida

Library of Congress Cataloging-in-Publication Data
Leite, John S.
   Successful parenting : a common sense guide to raising your teenag-
ers / John S. Leite, J. Kip Parrish.
      p.   cm.
   ISBN 1-55874-156-9
   1. Parent and teenager — United States. I. Parrish, J. Kip. II. Title.
   HQ799.15.L45   1991
649/.125—dc20

© 1991 John S. Leite and J. Kip Parrish
ISBN 1-55874-156-9

Publisher: Health Communications, Inc.
            3201 S.W. 15th Street
            Deerfield Beach, Florida 33442-8190

Acknowledgments

We would like to thank Pam and Terrye for their ongoing support, insights and contributions to our education about the importance of marriage and family.

Thanks to Ryan and Kellyn for their continuing willingness to give personalized instruction in the art of parenting.

Also, appreciation is extended to the Parrish children for their continuing efforts to make their parents acutely aware of the limits of parental control.

We would also like to thank the adolescents and their families with whom we have worked over the past 12 years. They have clearly taught us more about parenting than any book, class or professor. Also we would like to thank the staff at Charter Lakeside Hospital in Memphis, who have been family, friends and teachers to us for years.

Finally, we thank Sharon and Ed Hearn and especially Susan Clark for their dedication to education about addictions and their support of the book.

Contents

Preface

We admit it. We were wrong.

We thought that since we had survived adolescence ourselves and lived to tell about it, we must know something about it. We went to graduate school, took courses in child development and even taught classes on the subject. Surely this made us knowledgeable. Eventually, we received Ph.D.s and began working on an adolescent unit at a major hospital. Were we experts on the subject or what?

Unfortunately, it took about three minutes of working with an argumentative, manipulative, but very normal 13-year-old with an M.A. (Master of Adolescence) to let us know that all of our past training and experience were practically worthless when it came to understanding and effectively intervening in the lives of adolescents and their families.

Since we are willing to acknowledge our inadequacies, then hopefully you too are willing to admit that you don't feel like an expert and are, in fact, a little uncertain about how to approach the prospect of rearing an adolescent.

The following test is an opportunity for you to become more aware of your beliefs as a parent and to contrast them with the beliefs we have developed over the past 12 years. Respond as honestly as possible.

Good luck! (And be sure to use a Number 2 pencil.)

The Leite-Parrish Parenting IQ Test

Answer each question true or false:

1. An adolescent functions more like an adult than a child.

2. Such behaviors as smoking, drinking, lying and breaking rules are part of the normal stage of development called adolescence and therefore will resolve if parents are patient and understanding.

3. By using proper techniques, including love combined with discipline, parents can control their adolescents' behavior.

4. Adolescents who feel frustration, unhappiness and confusion have major problems. Parents need to respond with more praise, encouragement and reassurance.

5. The adolescent experience now is very different from that of most parents and parents therefore should not trust their own judgment and experience when making decisions about their adolescents.

6. Parents' first priority should be their children's happiness, regardless of the cost to themselves financially or emotionally.

7. Parents who really love their adolescents can also trust them.

8. By rewarding adolescents financially for good grades, parents help to build the value of education.

9. Adolescents need not be expected to become involved in situations that might cause feelings of embarrassment or insecurity.

10. Parents and adolescents should be friends.

11. Parents need to provide reasons and acceptable explanations when establishing rules or setting limits for adolescents.

12. Adolescents learn best from a disciplinary approach that gives them facts and lets them make their own decisions.

13. Effective communication is the key to most parent/adolescent problems.

14. On the issues of sex, drugs and music, adolescents should make their own choices without interference from parents.

Finished? We want to let you know, up front, that we understand how you feel when we tell you that we believe the correct answer to every question on the preceding quiz is false. And for every mistake you made as evidenced by a true answer, rest assured we made that same mistake, despite our education.

The good news is that we have wised up. We listened closely to the adolescents with whom we worked, and each one of them had an important lesson to teach us about their world. A professor once told us, "The only time you learn is when you listen, because what you have to say, you already know." We feel we have listened well and have been taught by the experts — thousands of adolescents.

More than anything else, our adolescent teachers have taught us that our society has gradually lost its ability, and perhaps its sense of obligation, to instill a stable foundation of basic positive values in its young people. Our culture thrives on the principles of materialism and immediate gratification. Missing are traditional beliefs in the intrinsic value of work and effort, in treating others the way we wish to be treated and the idea that freedom and privileges need to be earned through mature, responsible living.

Our approach reflects the spirit of these values and the belief that healthy parents can trust their instincts and assume that, in the vast majority of cases, their judgment is better than their adolescent child's. Parents are in the best position to set limits, guidelines and expectations for their adolescent children.

Our ideas are based upon sound psychological principles of adolescent child-rearing, while taking into account our fast-paced, ever-changing society. At the same time, it is a pragmatic, common-sense approach. We do not offer simplistic, catchy or cute techniques as a substitute for a basic philosophy of parenting. However, we by no means believe that we have provided a comprehensive, exhaustive discussion of the various topics presented. Entire books have been written on anyone of these areas. We have, with a little background thrown in for a frame of reference, distilled our own knowledge and experience down to an easily understood set of guidelines for parental and adolescent behavior.

Responsible, effective parenting is a lifelong commitment, not a hobby or a part-time job. This is not to say that parenting cannot be enjoyable. Many parents reminisce about early childhood days when their kids were fun to be around, implying, of course, that the good feelings end abruptly when kids enter adolescence. However, our experience has taught us that adolescents can provide just as much laughter, pride and satisfaction as younger children. When parents lose those positive feelings, it is not necessarily their adolescent's fault. Such a loss is often caused by parents' faulty goals and approaches. A primary purpose of this book, therefore, is to help parents enjoy life with their adolescents while at the same time fulfilling their commitment to guide their kids to maturity. We hope that a teenager's high school graduation night can feel just as good as a five-year-old's "I love you" at bedtime.

Introduction

Adolescents are easy to understand, right? After all, we all were teenagers once, so we must know all there is to know about adolescence. How many times have you said to your kids, "Don't forget, I was your age once"? While it seems incomprehensible to them that we have ever been anything other than grown-ups and hopelessly outdated, each of us has survived the adolescent years and carries a variety of memories into adulthood.

Survival of adolescence and the diminishing intensity of emotional memories are the key differences that separate us so frustratingly from our kids. We have survived adolescence and the experience has changed us in ways that remove us from ever being able to relate to our kids in a totally empathic and understanding manner. Our kids are evaluating us fairly accurately when they look at us bewildered and calmly say we just don't understand them. They have not yet survived their adolescence and it still remains a questionable proposition for them.

How is it that parents have so much difficulty understanding when they had to deal with the same developmental transition? Have you ever read a book for the second time and marveled at how much more you got out of it, how different the book seemed to you? Is the book different? Did you really miss that much the first time or had you forgotten the very thing that you see as so different now? No, the book hasn't changed and it isn't that you felt the same way then and have forgotten it all. The fact is *you* are different. You have grown, matured and experienced things that changed who you are in subtle ways. Typically, these changes are imperceptible to you, but may be more obvious to others.

Dealing with teenagers provides a similar experience. Armed with the knowledge that we once were adolescents, it is easy to feel we are picking up a book we recognize instantly and remember well. Aren't we amazed, then, when we are faced with creatures who seem so out of touch with the real world, who see the world from a perspective so different from our own? Often we deny the difference in perception that kids maintain and view them as resistant, oppositional and rebellious — when in fact their behavior is quite consistent with their view of the world and their experience.

Imagine you have hopped a plane to France to attend a business meeting. Your assignment is to negotiate a contract with someone who only speaks French while you speak only English. To work out the contract, you are expected to teach him English, but have been warned that he is patriotic and has little motivation to learn another language. But, negotiation and effective interaction require common understanding of language, knowledge of the other's perspective of the world, clearly defined expectations and an understanding of the history that led to the development of the situation at hand. Chances are, you will feel quite frustrated in your attempt to teach English to this Frenchman and accomplish your goal, and will come to view your counterpart as resistant and oppositional. This is similar to your task as parents trying to relate to your adolescents.

To understand teenagers fully and set the stage for the best relationship possible, we need to be aware of several important factors, including who adolescents are, how they view the world, and the nature of the society in which they are developing and, hopefully, maturing. Understanding how our current society came into existence is important in working effectively with kids, because the impact of this society on the development of kids is a critical factor. Adolescent issues are universal and have changed little over time. However, what adolescent issues can become attached to within society determines what we may see in kids as they struggle with developmental problems. A good knowledge of our current society and its history will help us in this quest.

For parents to develop theories and the associated techniques necessary for measuring and guiding adolescent behavior in the 1990s, they must understand initially the concept of adolescence as a developmental stage. Chapter One describes adolescence as a cultural term marking the biological transition from child to adult. This process is universal and reflects similar developmental issues the world over. It is the nature of our modern, industrialized society and its interaction with this process that makes this period unique, complex and confusing.

As a developmental stage, adolescence is accompanied by various psychological characteristics consistent with immature development. Chapter Two describes adolescence in terms of self-perception, thinking, defense mechanisms, values, sexuality and socialization.

It is Chapter Three, however, that sets the stage for the specific ideas and techniques critical to effective parenting. Here we discuss recent changes in society that have so drastically altered adolescent experience. Massive changes in the institutions of education, government, religion and the media are described in terms of their inability to provide clear, consistent values for young people. Similarly, drastic changes in public attitudes toward drug use, sexuality and materialism are discussed as they impact the maturation process. Even more importantly, tremendous changes in the basic structure of today's family systems are highlighted because these changes have a direct impact on the amount of structure available in the parenting process.

Armed with this information, readers are ready to focus upon basic principles of effective parenting. However, as a prerequisite to teaching effective principles, readers are challenged to examine myths and false assumptions that obstruct healthy parenting.

Finally, we present our basic principles, the 10 Commandments Of Healthy, Effective Parenting. These principles result from combining intensive psychological training with many years of experience with adolescents and their families. They represent a common-sense approach to parenting, which is applicable to a wide variety of situations. To further demonstrate these principles and their application, we have included questions and answers typical of parent/adolescent problems. An Appendix includes a glossary of adolescent terms, a list of the signs of adolescent drug use, a behavioral contract (which also helps parents apply these principles to specific situations), a list of warning signs of unhealthy parental attitudes and behavior, and a checklist for serious adolescent depression.

1

Adolescence: A Stage
Of Childhood

Sandra Segretti is running late for work again. As she drives, she reflects upon how tired she is from staying up late every night all week to help her son, Tony, work on his term paper. She knows that as a senior in high school, he must complete the project this week to graduate. Sandra feels particularly frustrated because while she is typing and trying to finish the paper, Tony is talking on the phone and seems concerned only with getting a date for the senior prom. He pays excessive attention to arrangements for picking up his tuxedo but is unconcerned about misspelled words in his paper. She cannot understand why Tony does not seem to realize there will be no graduation if he does not finish this paper and pass this course. Why is Tony, at six feet tall, fully grown, acting so immaturely and irresponsibly?

Mrs. Segretti is making a common mistake. She is assuming that because Tony looks like an adult and is 17 years old, he will think and act like an adult. Because she unconsciously expects Tony to act like an adult, she is confused when he acts like what he is, a developing child.

Adolescence needs to be viewed as a stage of childhood, not adulthood. Defined strictly, adolescence is the transition from childhood to adulthood. As such, it is a universal process of development. The culture in which children develop determines both the length of time devoted to adolescence and the specific expectations of what must be accomplished during this period.

Here is an excellent description of adolescence by a knowledgeable adult who writes:

> Of bodily desires it is the sexual to which they are most disposed to give way and in regard to sexual desire they exercise no self-restraint . . . They are passionate, irascible and apt to be carried away by their impulses . . . Youth is the age when people are most devoted to their friends or relations or companions . . . If the young commit a fault, it is always on the side of excess and exaggeration . . . For they carry everything too far, whether it be their love or hatred or anything else.

Whereas these words could easily have been written by one of today's parents, they were written by the Greek philosopher, Aristotle, over 2300 years ago.

Although adolescence has always reflected emotional and impulsive behavior, historically, it has been quite brief and ceremonial in nature. The length of time devoted to it loosely approximated the time it took for the physical changes that signal biological adulthood to occur. Young boys who survived biological puberty and showed outward signs of physical maturation were given the south 40 to plow and considered men. Their status was upgraded quickly, and generally they felt secure in this new position. Similarly, with the onset of puberty and menstruation, teenage girls were considered women and expected to marry and produce families. They too had new identities and were expected to be secure in their new roles and sense of status.

It's interesting to note that 100 years ago, puberty and physical maturation took place much later than it does today. And although children now become physically mature at an increasingly earlier age, social, emotional and intellectual maturity takes considerably longer than it did 100 years ago. In our highly complex technological society, it simply takes a person much longer to develop the skills needed for mature functioning. Today the adolescent quest for maturity and independence usually continues well into the mid-twenties. Even then, it is not unusual to see in our culture "adolescents" of 35, 40 or 45 years of age.

Adolescence, therefore, is an extremely confusing concept for kids as well as parents to understand. Society says that at age 18, adolescents have reached adulthood and are legally emancipated. Yet they cannot purchase alcohol until they are 21. They also have difficulty borrowing money from a bank or purchasing anything on credit until at least age 21. At 18, many adolescents are only two-thirds of the way through their education and in no position to be financially independent. While most adolescents sincerely desire the adult privileges conferred at age 18, few are as desirous of the responsibilities.

On the most basic level, successfully completing adolescence needs to prepare individuals for living effectively in the adult world. While trapped in the transition from childhood to adulthood, adolescents confront several rather specific developmental tasks. The abilities to engage in goal-directed behavior, to delay gratification, to tolerate frustration and to control impulses are required for successful passage. Similarly, establishing a positive self-identity is also a major task of adolescence. In addition, adolescent issues include preparing for separation from family and developing confidence in their ability to meet the demands of the world.

Simply put, adolescence ends when individuals have gained maturity, which we like to define as the willingness to do what is best, even when what is best is different from what is wanted. How often individuals choose what is best defines their level of maturity. Two-year-olds pursue wants almost exclusively and this is normal. Age and maturity increase the ratio of choosing what is best to choosing wants. This definition fits those 15 or 50 years of age and illustrates the essence of the adolescent process, which is developing the ability to separate childish wants from actual needs. This definition also takes into account the role of society in determining what behavior is appropriate.

In summary, adolescence is a universal phenomenon, and as a developmental process, it has been occurring in the same way for thousands of years. Effectively managing adolescent behavior requires an understanding of this process as well as the psychological characteristics that accompany this stage of development.

2

The Psychological World Of Adolescents

Adolescents As Aliens

It is 5:00 p.m. and the countdown has begun. Susan, age 16, is preparing herself for a big date. After 30 minutes of fluffing, puffing, rolling and twisting the sacred hair, she is now ready to begin the makeup ritual. But first, Susan decides to get a Diet Coke. At this point, tragedy strikes.

Reaching for the pause that refreshes, she catches a nail on the mayonnaise jar. "Crack!" The sound seemingly can be heard for blocks.

Susan shrieks and screams and then runs to her room, slamming the door behind her. She throws herself onto the bed sobbing. From behind the door come instructions to call her boyfriend and say she is sick. She cannot possibly be seen in public with a broken nail.

Susan's mother is totally perplexed. She has never understood this endless series of unpredictable episodes.

Unable to make sense out of her daughter's behavior she sighs and says to herself in exasperation, "She's like an alien from another planet."

This description of teenagers as aliens is probably more accurate than most, because it reflects the fact that adolescent behavior does not fit into adult conceptualizations of how normal people are "supposed" to act. Adolescents don't act like children, but they sure don't act like adults. They do seem to be from an alien planet or, at best, some remote foreign land, which has its own customs, dress and language. A more appropriate name for these alien adolescent Americans might be *Adolericans.*

Many frustrated parents view adolescence as a disease only time can cure. *Adolitis* is characterized by dramatic abnormalities in speech, attitudes and behavior. In most cases, remission of Adolitic symptoms occurs in approximately ten years. Until this remission, it has been suggested that the only sensible approach to the situation is to bury these diseased children in time capsules and dig them up ten years later.

Since society has not developed a space shuttle capable of deporting Adolericans, and until General Motors develops a good time capsule, parents are left with the task of trying to understand adolescents.

While most theorists and researchers define adolescence as the transition from childhood to adulthood, it is an ongoing stage of childhood, not adulthood. One of the more common complaints is that adolescents act so "immature." Parents continue to be shocked and surprised when adolescent family members look like adults but act like children. In fact, adolescents are much more like children than adults. Adolescents are developing but not fully formed individuals and still have very childish ways of thinking, feeling and acting. The alien behavior reflected in adolescence is typical immaturity.

Parents tend to measure adolescent behavior with an adult yardstick, operating under the mistaken assumption that they understand adolescence because they have been through it. But the mere fact of having survived this pro-

cess and having entered parenthood and adulthood neces-
sitates their having developed a style of thinking and feeling distinctly different from those of adolescents. Using
an adult perspective when attempting to understand and
manage adolescent behavior is like trying to repair foreign
cars with American tools that look appropriate but don't
quite fit. Making the adjustment from an adult perspective
to that of an adolescent is extremely frustrating, similar
to the process of learning to calculate measurements in
meters, grams and liters, rather than miles, ounces and
quarts. Parents are much less frustrated and considerably
more effective when they adequately understand the nature of the individuals with whom they are working.

The Search For Identity

Although Linda Thompson is home from work first,
she is happy to wait for her husband's arrival before con-
ducting the daily roomcheck of her 14-year-old son's inner
sanctum. As Ron Thompson enters the room and the
inspection begins, Linda can't help but notice the incredible contrast between Ron, dressed in a suit and tie, and
the posters lining the walls of the "sacred room," particularly those of her son's most recent objects of worship.
She cannot understand how Zach can actually look up to
these rock stars who look more like women than men.
She has forgotten, of course, how strange her wire-
rimmed glasses and bell-bottoms looked to her parents
when she was this age. Instead she wonders, "What makes
my son think this way?"

Developmental theorists, from Sigmund Freud to Erik
Erikson, have generally agreed that a primary goal or task
of adolescence is to form an identity. A related term,
"individuation," refers to the struggle to separate adolescent values and behaviors from those of parents. However, when psychologists use these terms in an attempt to
help parents understand their adolescent's behavior, parents respond with blank stares. Theories sound good, but

applying them to actual behavior is difficult. Thus, while the concept of individuation is an important component of the adolescent experience, it needs to be understood in terms of how it is reflected in the actual thinking, feeling and behavior of adolescents.

To gain identity, adolescents have to distinguish and define themselves as different from others. To do this, adolescents must be recognized or given attention that confirms their separateness. A common means of accomplishing this goal is the process of divergence. Put simply, the best way to be noticed is to be different. For purposes of understanding adolescents, Descarte's famous axiom, "I think, therefore I am," can be rewritten to, "I am noticed, therefore I am." In effect, adolescents use divergent behavior in an attempt to get attention and define their separateness.

Whereas little six-year-old Johnny might climb to the top of the refrigerator and say, "Look at me, Mommy," adolescent John shows only a slight modification of this process by coming home with a strange haircut and unusual clothing. The message is still a variation of "Look at me, Mommy," but John is also trying to say "I'm different from you." And of course, the best way to make divergent statements is to think or act in ways that are very different from accepted adult values. In today's society, adolescents are drawn to making divergent statements through their choices in clothing, music, language and attitudes, which frequently reflect themes of sexuality, adventure and experimentation.

Making a divergent statement as a means of gaining recognition and establishing identity in adolescence is not new. Many adults still remember the shock and horror of American society when adolescents became flappers in the 1920s. Certainly every '50s parent feared that their teenagers would become sex-crazed, maniacal beasts after watching just one performance of Elvis the Pelvis. However, in the '30s, '40s and '50s, adolescents could make divergent statements by deviating only slightly from prevailing beliefs in a relatively stable and conservative society. But beginning in the '60s, American society as a whole became increasingly more open to freedom of expression. In an atmosphere of increased flexibility and tolerance of "different strokes for different folks," as Sly and the Family Stone sang, more deviation from a broader norm seemed necessary to send the message, "I'm different." Long hair, drug use, political rebellion and "turning on, tuning in and dropping out" (to paraphase Timothy Leary) became prominent means of making divergent statements. In today's society, which permits even more freedom of individual expression, making a divergent statement can require even more deviant behavior.

Again, using music as an example, look at what rock bands must do to gain an adolescent following. Elvis had to swing his hips, the Beatles grew their hair, but the current crop of heavy metal and rock stars utilize satanic symbols, violence, profanity and graphic sexuality as a means of departing from accepted adult values and customs.

With today's permissiveness, adolescents may feel a need to become increasingly unusual and extreme in their behavior in an attempt to make a statement. While the vast majority of kids are able to make divergent statements in appropriate ways without causing themselves or others great harm, this quest can easily turn destructive if appropriate parental structure and limits are not in place.

Self-Esteem

"I'll Study Later, Mom. Where Is My New Eye Shadow?"

Parents are frequently quite concerned about their adolescent's self-esteem and with good reason. Low self-esteem is a major source of problem behavior in adolescents. We define positive self-esteem as seeing oneself as a confident, effective, worthwhile individual who generally acts in successful ways with his or her physical, social and emotional environment. Positive self-esteem comes from successful interaction with the environment. For younger children, the primary environment revolves around security in their families and parental approval. Adolescents, given their need to form a separate identity, shift to an interaction with their peer environment. In a sense, all adolescents have low self-esteem, because their self-evaluation must occur within the framework of developmental growth, limited experience and an ambiguous status — neither child nor adult. Because they are in a state of extreme change, they tend to feel insecure and inadequate. At some level, most adolescents are aware of their shortcomings and this ambiguous status. As such, they rarely feel confident or in control. Much of adolescence is spent attempting to acquire a feeling of mastery and status.

To acquire self-esteem, a shift must occur from a sense of self based on external validation to one based on internal validation.

That is, adolescent self-esteem comes not from hearing, "You're a good person," but rather from an internal belief of "I am a good person." However, these internal beliefs are based upon feedback from the external environment.

Many adolescents are able to attain this sense of confidence and self-worth through achievement in academics, sports or music. Others use jobs (much like adults), as a means of feeling important. Some gain feelings of self-esteem from adopting a personality style in which they are very helpful and supportive of others.

Unfortunately, these kinds of self-esteem boosters tend to take considerable time and require much dedication, patience and hard work. Since adolescence is typically characterized by impulsivity, the majority of adolescents are not particularly long on these qualities and frequently look for simpler, less time-consuming solutions to their underlying feelings of insecurity. Thus, rather than waiting for long-term gains derived from achievement, or merely waiting for these long-term rewards to occur, adolescents frequently try to feel good and worthwhile the easy way, seeking a quick fix.

One of the most common quick fixes is reliance upon materialism. Adolescents accumulate various types of "stuff," which attests to their status and importance. Cars, clothing, stereos and other adolescent toys gain value at a psychological level. Feeling good becomes an issue of what they have, as opposed to who they are. Contrary to what most parents attempt to teach, the motto becomes "It's what's on the outside that counts." "Stuff" therefore, becomes very important to adolescents, and these material possessions must be the right name-brand or model to make the right status statement to the right group — the one an adolescent is attempting to join. Adolescents often feel so desperate in their desire to have the right kind of stuff that these desires become "needs" — necessary for survival in the adolescent culture. Material things supply status and acceptance as well as fun and offer temporary relief from underlying insecurities.

Adolescents also commonly cope with underlying low self-esteem by acting in a manner that makes them feel more adult or grown-up. Unfortunately, logic, responsibility or hard work are not usually the adult characteristics adolescents assume for self-esteem enhancement. Instead, they often pick out the seemingly glamorous but not always healthy aspects of adult functioning, which they believe are indicative of maturity (perhaps because they are forbidden to all but adults). This often is the impetus behind smoking, drug and alcohol use and sexual activity. The common increase in profanity by adolescents is part of this attempt to act and feel grown up.

Obviously, many of these premature statements of adulthood can quickly become destructive if appropriate parental limits are not set and consequences not provided for violation. Similarly, parents can respond to increases in responsible behavior by increasing an adolescent's level of freedom and opportunity for self-determined choice-making.

An adolescent's primary means of dealing with low self-esteem is identification with the youth culture, the peer group. This identification is frequently reflected in statements such as the following:

I had to, Mom. I didn't want to be a nerd.
Oh Dad, I'll be the only one there who is with his parents.
If I can't drive the car to the party, I'm just not going.
I'll just die if I don't get into that group.

Whereas each of these statements is capable of striking fear in the hearts of the most confident of parents, they merely reflect a normal human need to affiliate with others as a means of gaining feelings of acceptance and status. History demonstrates clearly that long before *homo sapiens* existed, almost all species were characterized by the tendency to band together in groups for protection and survival. With the dawn of man, not only was physical protection offered by group affiliation, but psychological and emotional protection as well. The point is that humans are very social by nature and influenced and motivated by social variables.

Parents, you too are heavily influenced by your friends in more ways than you realize. Do you, Mom, consider what everyone else is wearing before you dress for a party? Do you, Dad, ever think about trading in your not-so-late model car, which runs fine but looks out of style, because of what your friends and neighbors are driving? If you answer yes, you too are responding to peer pressure.

What makes the adolescent need to belong so strong? Humans are basically insecure. There is a lot of responsibility in the world, but limited personal control. The physical, emotional and sexual changes that accompany adolescence create a tremendous sense of internal chaos. This unstable state is compounded by television, music, parents and school, all of which give out inconsistent messages about what is good and what is right. Adolescents become like drowning men, clinging tightly to whatever they can grab. Peer acceptance is the salve that soothes and heals adolescent pain. Friendship makes adolescents feel better.

Children first learn to feel important and special in response to acceptance and support from parents.

As adolescents, they begin to separate and distance themselves from parents, losing the sense of security and acceptance they enjoyed as younger kids. At the same time, they have not yet learned to value themselves independently as individuals. Peer groups become a temporary, stopgap means of receiving reinforcement and support until individuals can gain this from successful interaction with the environment, which comes much later.

Most adolescent peer groups have one thing in common: They are different from adult and children's groups. Adolescent peer groups tend to occupy vague positions on a continuum ranging from positive/constructive values to negative/destructive values. Whereas the names and composition of groups vary to some degree depending upon geographic area, socio-economic group and the particular school, each group usually has relatively specific codes, laws and membership criteria. These values are displayed through various symbols in the form of clothing, music, language, attitudes and behavior.

Most of the time, peer groups are positive in their purpose and effect upon adolescent behavior. However, it is the negative effects of the grouping process with which parents are most familiar and concerned. To hear some parents talk, peer pressure is some type of horrible disease. "Peerus pressuritis" is seen as an affliction that conjures up fantasies of terror, fear and more horror than a slasher movie. However, the normal adolescent need for peer affiliation does not necessarily have to be viewed as dangerous, especially if it is approached in a logical and consistent manner.

Adolescents also attempt to validate themselves and raise their self-esteem by becoming involved with the opposite sex. These relationships have an extremely important developmental purpose: They provide basic information concerning the adolescent's masculinity or femininity. These relationships also help them to feel more mature and grown-up, while allowing them to make the self-statement, "If a member of the opposite sex likes me, I must be okay."

In general, early adolescent opposite-sex relationships tend to be superficial and based upon appearances. They are usually quite self-serving, as most adolescents are more concerned about gratifying their own needs, than actually caring about or providing a sense of security for others. These relationships are characterized by frequent change, thus providing a kind of laboratory in which adolescents begin to learn what types of interactions result in positive rather than negative feelings. Despite the superficiality and changeability, they can be very intense and emotional. This intensity underlies such statements as "I'm in love, it will last forever," or "If we break up, I'll die."

Unfortunately, these relationships can acquire addictive qualities. In these situations, adolescents attach themselves to members of the opposite sex in all-or-none attempts to gain a sense of security and self-worth. Thus, an adolescent's entire identity becomes invested in a relationship, and that relationship essentially controls the adolescent's entire existence. These types of relationships can become destructive and are frequent causes of serious behavioral and emotional problems ranging from drug abuse to suicide. Our approach is designed to help parents become aware of destructive opposite-sex relationships and to intervene *before* such relationships have negative effects upon adjustment.

In summary, low self-esteem is a normal state in which young people stumble through trial and error toward a more confident, self-secure level of functioning. Improved self-esteem, associated with maturity, reflects a gradual shift from external to internal validation of self-worth. In making this transition, adolescents rely heavily upon material things, *acting* grown-up, peer acceptance and opposite-sex relationships.

Adolescence As A Thinking Disorder

We recently recalled the story of the 15-year-old boy who stood on a busy street corner in downtown Memphis, looking very serious and intent, furiously waving two flags over his head. When a policeman asked what he was doing, he replied, "I'm waving these flags to scare off all the lions and tigers. Otherwise, they would eat me up." "But this is downtown Memphis. There are no lions and tigers out here," said the officer. The teen replied smugly, "It works real good, doesn't it?"

Adolescents carry around beliefs and assumptions about the world like those flags described above, seldom stopping to test those assumptions or validate their reality. Reality is based on subjective perception, not on objective facts or evidence. Because adolescence is a period of intense emotional upheaval, these emotions color their perception of the world and, therefore, their interpretation of reality.

Researchers like Jean Piaget say that adolescents are capable of rational, logical thought. But even though the potential for logical thought exists, it can be activated only through experience, of which adolescents have comparatively very little. Adolescent brains are like sophisticated, highly modernized computers with yet-to-be-developed programs. Without experience (the program), computers cannot consistently generate logical, relevant information. Even worse, adolescents often think they are mental giants and trust their own judgment more than that of parents or other adults. To understand adolescent behavior, parents must understand "normal" adolescent thinking and perception, which is characterized by a number of distortions, errors, fallacies and inconsistencies. In reviewing the major types of adolescent thinking errors, we are convinced that adolescence can be more easily understood as a thinking disorder.

Emotional Reasoning

I feel like a failure, I'll never be anybody.

This thinking error, particularly frustrating to parents, occurs when adolescents automatically assume that feelings are facts. These feelings influence the perceptual process and may distort reality. Adults know that feelings often lie. Time and experience teach that feelings can mislead. Mature people examine, explore and sort out feelings, often discovering that "this too shall pass." In contrast, adolescents typically act immediately upon feelings, mistakenly thinking that they reflect reality. The adolescent quoted above felt like a failure after receiving an F. He decided since he was a failure that there was no use in studying or trying in school anymore.

In many such situations, parents or adults attempt to point out to emotionally reasoning adolescents various "facts" that indicate the feeling does not accurately reflect the truth. However, presenting objective facts has little impact on emotionally aroused adolescents and their persistent beliefs. This is why the principles and communication techniques embodied in our Ten Commandments are so important. Unfortunately, suicidal behavior is frequently a result of this thinking error, as adolescents attempt permanent solutions — killing themselves — to transient situational problems based upon short-term feelings of sadness, loss or worthlessness.

Emotional reasoning is also apparent in cases of adolescents who have new boyfriends or girlfriends, feel infatuation, conclude that it is love and that since it's love, it will last forever. They then may become sexually involved and later feel devastated when such relationships end. Adolescents tend not only to think that their feelings are facts, but they further reason that these present feelings will continue into the future, thus making situational feelings seem even more overwhelming.

The Stage-Fright Phenomenon

> I won't wear glasses. They make me look like a nerd.

Adolescents often irrationally assume that everyone, especially peers, are constantly watching and judging them. They think they are always on stage, watched by some imaginary audience. This thinking error accounts for the all-consuming preoccupation with appearance, as evidenced by constant primping, clothes-changing and mirror-gazing. The fallacy of this distorted thinking would be obvious if adolescents were able to see things realistically. If most adolescents are constantly preoccupied with how they look and what they themselves are doing, how could they possibly pay any attention to what everyone else is doing? Insecurity and low self-esteem tend to make adolescents extremely self-conscious. They seem paranoid and magnify others' judgments and evaluations of themselves. They then make decisions based on these distorted perceptions.

Tunnel Vision

I'm stupid. I got a D on my report card.

Certainly a D is no academic triumph, but the rest of the grades, all As and Bs, were not even mentioned.

Tunnel vision occurs when adolescents select only certain aspects of experience to focus upon and "filter out" all other relevant aspects of their experience. This adolescent seized upon the one low grade on her report card and felt badly about herself while ignoring many other good grades. While this thinking style is common to all adolescents, it is particularly common in adolescents with low self-esteem who are especially sensitive about certain aspects of their personality, body, intelligence or social relationships. For example, adolescents often think they are ugly and have no friends, and no amount of parental encouragement or statements to the contrary seem to get past the negative filter. This creates a need for the special communication skills described later. Parents frequently try to counter adolescent perceptions with facts and are amazed and frustrated by the persistence of feelings produced by tunnel vision. Tunnel vision also occurs in adolescents who "know it all" and view only their strengths and virtues, but are unaffected by any feedback or information related to problems, weaknesses or inadequacies.

Extremism

At my school everybody is either a druggie or a prep.

This relatively common adolescent thinking error comes from the tendency to perceive events only in extremes of black and white. This is evident in adolescent perceptions of one parent as the "good guy," while the other parent is the "bad guy." Often the same parent will be viewed as totally good and loving one day, and then totally bad and hated the next. In terms of self-perception, an adolescent may view herself in one situation as the most stunning, confident and attractive person on earth. Moments later the bubble bursts and she sees herself as grotesquely ugly and inadequate.

This polarized manner of thinking is also illustrated when adolescents perceive all peers as fitting into one of only a few categories such as freaks, geeks or preps. In terms of language, this thinking error is reflected in the use of such words as "always," "never," "everybody," "nobody," and various other extreme, absolute terms. There is no middle ground. This style of thinking often causes dramatic mood swings.

Jumping To Conclusions

I didn't make the team. I can't do anything right.

Adolescents are jumping to conclusions when they incorrectly make generalizations based upon one piece of data. An adolescent boy believes he is ugly and worthless just because one girl refuses to go out with him. This type of overgeneralized thinking is exemplified when adolescents begin to truly believe their parents do not care about them because occasionally parents say no and refuse to let adolescents do something they really want to do. Adolescents frequently say things like, "All the cool people drink beer," when in fact, only some cool people do. Jumping to conclusions, like all adolescent thinking distortions, tends to result in over-sensitivity and emotional reactions out of proportion to the situation.

Self-Righteous Delusions

You just don't understand. You're trying to run my life.

Adolescents tend to believe that their own perceptions and impressions are absolutely correct and superior to those of all other people around them, especially adults. Whereas preadolescent children tend to accept that their parents are more knowledgeable and intelligent than they, adolescents enter a phase in which they automatically assume their parents know nothing, and only they possess the truth. This particular thinking error is probably the cause of more parental head-banging and hair-pulling than any other. In their infinite wisdom, adolescents decide they know best about boyfriends/girlfriends, peers, driving, how to wear clothes and most everything else. Of course, any attempt by parents or other adults to intrude into this highly organized delusional system is met with that famous phrase, "You just don't understand." While it may be true that parents do not fully comprehend their adolescent's position, adolescents are usually just frustrated because their parents do not agree with them. What adolescents really mean is, "You don't see it and accept it my way."

If it were not bad enough that adolescents think that their beliefs about themselves are accurate and absolutely correct, they then gauge their parents' intellectual ability by how often parental beliefs match their own. This often results in parents receiving a daily barrage of instructions and criticisms regarding how out-of-touch they are.

Such pseudo-intellectualism on the part of adolescents often spills over into the area of morality. Adolescents

many times become self-appointed experts in the areas
of honesty, freedom, religion and responsibility. In fact,
they believe that they know better than anyone else about
what is fair, and they frequently interpret anything that
is different from what they want as unfair. This particular thinking error fills much of the parent/child interaction of this period with countless arguments and verbal
sparring matches.

The Superman Syndrome

It won't happen to me.

Consistent with the belief that their intellectual skills
are highly developed, adolescents also tend to believe that
they are invincible and invulnerable to injury, pain or
negative consequences. Typically, adolescents may choose
not to wear seatbelts because they think seatbelts are not
"cool," but also because adolescents believe that car wrecks
happen to other people, never to them. Or they might
further reason that even if they were in an accident, they
would be magically thrown free from the crash, therefore
not needing a seatbelt anyway.

In a similar vein, adolescents often reason that only other
girls get pregnant and only other teenagers overdose or
become addicted. How many parents can relate to their
teenagers believing that they can magically graduate from
high school, attend the college of their choice and become
wildly successful, yet not have to study and make decent
grades? The Superman Syndrome is characterized by extreme naivete and an inability to understand that behavior
has very definite and usually predictable consequences.

To summarize, although adolescents may appear very
grown-up and mature, their thinking remains quite childish and immature. Fortunately, this situation is not termi-
nal, and adolescent thinking gradually becomes more logical
and adult-like as individuals gain age and experience. However, while this process is occurring, it is extremely impor-

tant that parents understand the nature of these adolescent thinking distortions. This understanding can then be incorporated into an effective approach to managing and structuring an adolescent's experience, a process we define as parenting.

Defense Mechanisms

After two weeks of agonizing, Brian has finally worked up the courage to ask the long-admired object of his fantasies to share prom night with him. Fortunately, she accepts. But only a week before the prom, after Brian has already spent his savings on a tuxedo rental, she tells him that she will be out of town that day and cannot go. The situation is made worse when Brian finds out that she actually received another offer from a different boy and will be attending another prom on the same night. Brian's parents know he is feeling embarrassment, humiliation and rejection. However, rather than coming home and ventilating these understandable feelings to his parents, he instead protects his relatively weak and insecure ego by using one or a combination of the following adolescent defense mechanisms.

Essentially, a defense mechanism is an unconscious psychological process that distorts the individual's perception of events to minimize feelings of inferiority, inadequacy, guilt or emotional pain. In moderation, defense mechanisms have constructive, positive functions, especially for adolescents dealing with the insecurity and uncertainty that are a normal part of growing up. In excess, however, they can also serve to severely distort an individual's perception in ways that result in self-destructive behavior. In general, these defense mechanisms have very useful, face-saving functions for adolescents, yet they tend to be a constant source of wonder to observing parents.

Denial

> It doesn't bother me. I don't know what everyone is
> worried about, it's no problem.

Consistent with these statements, Brian goes about his daily activities as if the rejection to go to the prom has never occurred. Brian's parents are amazed because he seems to be oblivious to what happened, and he shows no evidence of experiencing any of the expected negative feelings. Quite simply, Brian is in denial. He has refused to accept or acknowledge any of the painful feelings the situation seems to warrant. Denial is very different from lying, because in the case of denial, adolescents actually believe their own explanations, rather than merely trying to deceive others and avoid the negative consequences associated with the truth. Because adolescents are so often inexperienced and uncomfortable with the process of dealing with emotional pain, many times they simply block the awareness of it and act as if the situation did not exist. The greater the pain, the stronger the level of denial. On a mild level, adolescents often deny feelings of anger, rejection, inadequacy and inferiority. In more excessive forms, this need to deny can reach the point of absurdity where individuals refuse to look at such glaringly obvious problems as drug abuse, extreme sexual misconduct or self-destructive behavior.

Rationalization

> I really didn't like her that much anyway. The prom is
> for nerds and preps. None of the cool people are going.

With this statement, Brian is engaging in the relatively well-known defensive process of rationalization. In denial, individuals deny outright having problems or negative feelings related to an event. In rationalization, individuals explain away the severity of problems or feelings. Rationalization can take many forms. In minimization, adolescents say, "It may be a problem, but it's really not all that bad." Other common means of rationalizing guilt and avoiding self-blame include, "Everybody else does it," "I was in a bad mood," "I didn't mean to." As a way of dealing with feelings of hurt and rejection, a particular favorite of adolescents is, "It doesn't hurt, because I don't care." The sting of negative feedback can easily be avoided by thinking, "It doesn't apply to me." In essence, rationalization helps individuals reduce, or at times totally avoid, internal negative consequences or feelings associated with their behavior or experience.

Externalization

> I knew she'd change her mind because girls never really care about guys. They're just out for themselves.

By viewing girls in general as having the problem, Brian is able to avoid finding fault with himself, thus avoiding negative feelings of hurt and rejection. Blaming and projecting responsibility onto others is clearly one of the most common defense mechanisms among adolescents. Adolescents are frequently much better at finding fault with others than with accepting responsibility for their own problems, weaknesses and feelings. (Of course, adults never do this!)

From an adolescent perspective, poor grades are obviously the fault of teachers who "never explain anything" rather than of adolescents lacking attention, concentration or motivation to learn. Similarly, adolescents prefer to label their parents as unrealistic, expecting too much, too strict, unfair and old-fashioned, rather than looking at their own difficulty in accepting limits, complying with authority, and accepting responsibility for their choices. Obviously, if adolescents can successfully blame others in their own minds, then they do not have to feel guilty or wrong. Instead, adolescents tend to view themselves as innocent victims of horribly unfair and abusive situations in which they are made to suffer needlessly. When adolescents rely heavily upon the mechanism of externalization, it is often accompanied by feelings of self-pity and victimization. These two emotional companions to the externalization process can be recognized in such self-statements as "Poor me," "It's so awful," and "Look how you made me suffer." Brian therefore spends a great deal of time whining, pouting and moping and collects maximum amounts of sympathy and attention to soothe his "misery."

Acting Out

I hate you, and when I turn 18, I'm out of here.

This statement is one of several screamed by Brian in response to a simple question about whether he had taken out the trash that afternoon. Basically Brian is acting out and displacing his feelings of hurt and anger associated with the prom rejection toward his parents, who are much more accessible and accepting targets of his negative feelings than the rejecting female peer. This particular type of defensive reaction is often employed by adolescents when the previously described defensive processes fail to successfully reduce internal pressure and negative feelings. Individuals simply act, usually impulsively, in an attempt to avoid, ventilate or escape underlying unpleasant feelings. In a mild form, acting out is often evident in tantrums, arguments, yelling and picking fights with other family members. In more severe forms, acting out as a defense mechanism is evidenced in more destructive behaviors such as running away, drug abuse, aggression and destruction of property.

In general, whereas the use of defense mechanisms is in many ways a very positive and constructive process, the excessive and rigid use of these defense mechanisms prevents individuals from appropriately experiencing reality and its consequences, a reality that unfortunately includes feelings of hurt, inadequacy, fear, failure and anger. If individuals constantly distort their experience, they never learn to successfully cope with, master, accept or understand their feelings and behavior, and they can, therefore, never change those parts of themselves that are undesirable or harmful, or enhance those aspects of themselves that they admire. We often tell adolescents that if they don't deal with their feelings, their feelings will deal with them. For maturation to occur, adolescents must learn to see themselves as they really are. Only then can they begin the process of accepting responsibility for changing themselves — not others — into caring, honest and productive individuals whom they truly like and respect.

Values And Morality

Why Good Kids Do Bad Things

It is 10:00 p.m. at the Brown home and a confrontation is in full progress. Mr. and Mrs. Brown have just discovered that their daughter, LaDonna, has lied to them. Before leaving the house, she told them she would only be going to the mall, but after she got there, she and her friends snuck into an X-rated movie, something she knew her parents would not approve of. The Browns are shocked, hurt and angry because their 15-year-old daughter — who was always such an honest and compliant person before becoming a teenager — seems to have taken a turn toward dishonesty. What's more, she does not seem to feel any remorse or guilt when she is caught. What happened to the "good" LaDonna?

The concept of morality in developing adolescents is often very confusing and difficult for parents to understand. Parents are frequently shocked and surprised when formerly compliant, honest and responsible children behave disobediently, dishonestly, manipulatively or irresponsibly. In response to such behavior, parents often feel hurt, personally rejected and like failures as parents. Yet many times, this immoral behavior is understandable if it is regarded in terms of extremely immature and emerging systems of adolescent values.

By definition, values are internal rules or codes of conduct. These internal rules obviously have a tremendous impact on individual behavior. In large part, people act as they believe.

In early years, children are primarily motivated by external consequences. Young children are honest, responsible and obedient because this type of behavior results in more privileges, less punishment and parental approval. Their behavior is directed more by external consequences than internal rules.

In the years prior to adolescence, children begin to develop early signs of internal attitudes and rules that govern behavior. However, internal rules at this time generally reflect the attitudes of parents, teachers and other influential adults. In childhood, kids live by rules not truly their own.

In adolescence, children feel a strong need to develop systems of standards and beliefs separate from their parents. In addition, adolescents no longer place as great an importance on parental approval but care more about peer approval instead. Since parental approval is no longer the primary standard by which adolescents judge their behavior, many other factors begin to influence the development of their values and subsequent behavior.

As noted previously, adolescents are heavily influenced by the institutions of which they are members, particularly schools and churches as well as families. But with the generalized decrease in the level of structure and consistency provided by today's institutions, adolescents receive many confusing messages about what is right. Similarly, they are given constant messages by the media that may conflict with what they have been taught by families and other institutions. Finally, in an attempt to resolve the disparity, they turn to peer groups as their primary guides. Unfortunately, peer groups are composed of individuals just as insecure, irrational and as immature as they are; definitely a situation of the blind leading the blind. So one reason for immoral behavior in adolescents is that they are somewhat void of stable, mature, personal values. They experience difficulty deciding what is right for them due to inconsistent messages received from institutions, media and peer groups. Another issue is that knowing right from wrong does not necessarily mean individuals actually can or will act in "right" ways. In fact, there are several other reasons why adolescents frequently act in inappropriate, immoral ways.

A major factor in an adolescent's immoral behavior is the previously described ability of adolescents to use the defense mechanism of rationalization. Thus, adolescents may easily justify lying to their parents by saying to themselves, "They were unfair to me, why should I be fair to them?" Similarly, kids often see themselves in a battle with parents over limits, so adolescents adopt the principle of *all's fair in love and war*. In this way, sneaking out at night to see someone of the opposite sex is no longer wrong to them.

Such adolescent thinking errors as the Superman Syndrome, in which adolescents reason "It won't happen to me," also contribute to adolescent immorality, especially when adolescents choose to smoke, drink, have sex, etc. In many cases adolescents know they will feel guilt or suffer negative consequences later, but they reason, "Well, that's tomorrow, and I'll worry about that then." In these situations, a naive, short-sighted, self-centered lack of regard for the emotional and practical consequences of an act leads to the negative behavior.

Perhaps the most common reason for immoral behavior in adolescents is their developing self-esteem and strong need for acceptance from peers. Even though they know it is wrong to go somewhere without permission, they will do so anyway, just to avoid feelings of peer rejection and low self-worth that would result from *doing what is right*.

Sometimes adolescents simply act before they think. Impulse turns into action and the whole process of deciding whether an act is right or wrong is bypassed due to an adolescent tendency toward impulsivity. This is particularly evident in the area of sexual behavior where hormones and the need to be liked and accepted frequently outweigh moral issues.

One activity characterized by high levels of immoral and antisocial behavior is alcohol and other drug use. In addition to making adolescents feel good, all of the commonly used drugs, including alcohol, tend to decrease inhibitions and suspend moral judgment. Drug-using adolescents are far more likely to show extreme departures from socially accepted behavior.

In summary, immoral behavior in adolescence is a reflection of attempts by immature, confused and incompletely formed individuals to balance what is fair, good and right against their own needs, desires and impulses. With this understanding, we will later recommend some very important techniques and principles to be utilized when managing this type of behavior.

Teenage Sexuality

"If You Love Me, You'll Do It"

Mrs. Cooper was cleaning out her 13-year-old daughter's room after she had given up on getting Teresa to do it herself. As she began to throw away several scraps of paper that looked like trash, she noticed that one of them had handwriting that did not belong to her daughter. Although she felt guilty about invading Teresa's privacy, she could not resist the temptation to read the note. She quickly wished she had never walked into her daughter's room, much less read anything, for the note was apparently from a young boy in Teresa's class and filled with fairly explicit sexual suggestions. The note alluded to getting together during the upcoming weekend, when Teresa was supposed to spend the night with a girlfriend. Mrs. Cooper was shocked to think of her daughter receiving this kind of note, much less being sexually active. She didn't know what to do. It seemed just yesterday her little girl was playing with dolls and dress-up clothes.

Sexual activity among adolescents is a reality with which most parents feel extremely uncomfortable. Research, public opinion polls and newspaper headlines suggest that adolescents become sexually active at an increasingly earlier age. Therefore, no description of adolescence is complete without a discussion of sexuality.

Whereas for centuries adolescence has been recognized as a time of sexual growth and maturation, sexuality for today's adolescent has also come to be associated with power, popularity, self-gratification and self-esteem. As we described earlier, the sexual revolution combined with big business has created an atmosphere of sexual preoccupation in today's society.

It is a well-known fact that hormones and sexual impulses are at an all-time high during puberty and the teenage years. And while many adolescent relationships are a function of one gland calling to another, our experience as psychologists has shown that adolescents feel much more pressure to perform sexually from the media and their peer groups than they do from the hormonal call of nature. Because of this pressure, adolescents engage in sexual activity at much earlier ages than only 20 years ago at the supposed height of the sexual revolution. Therefore, many adolescents are making decisions about sex when they are extremely immature . . . emotionally, socially and intellectually. The consequences of early sexual activity can be devastating. Although the most obvious external consequences are teenage pregnancy and sexually transmitted diseases, these are only two of the many consequences experienced by emotionally immature yet sexually active adolescents.

Strongly Linked To Emotion

Contrary to the notion popularized during the '60s that sexual behavior is detached from emotional intimacy, sex is not just an isolated form of self-gratification but is quite emotion-laden. Adolescents are very sensitive and protective of their bodies, as they should be, and those teenagers who are sexually active (especially girls), often experience significant underlying feelings of shame, guilt and low self-worth because sexuality remains one of the most taboo, anxiety-related topics in our culture. Whereas boys stereotypically use sex as a means of conquest, power, self-gratification and peer acceptance, adolescent girls are usually looking to the sexual act as a means of achieving security, intimacy and closeness. In some situations, adolescents appear to use sex as a means of satisfying emotional needs for nurturance and attention not being met elsewhere. Experts state that boys tend to use love to get sex, while girls tend to use sex to get love. At other times, sex seems to function as just another "quick fix" or "new toy" that produces a state of intense pleasure.

The sexual revolution that started in the '60s promised a liberation of values, attitudes and behavior. It's unrealized goal was to stimulate the emergence of unconflicted sexuality. However, what appears to have happened is a change in sexual behavior, while underlying values, beliefs and morals have shifted more slowly. Societal beliefs about sexuality have been fairly consistent for centuries and tend to resist rapid change. The continuing conflict between values and behavior gives rise to strong feelings of emotional turmoil in today's adolescents.

Let's face it, sex is fun and it feels good, and immaturity is marked by the pursuit of wants instead of what is best.

To summarize, adolescence is a stage of childhood. Adolescent thinking, feeling and experience are quite different from their adult counterparts. It is critical that parents understand the world of their adolescents before attempting to guide them to maturity.

3

Our Changing Society

It is Saturday morning and Bob Walton is getting a bad start on the weekend. Early on he had to deal with his 16-year-old daughter, Debbie, who had missed her curfew the night before. He and his wife were also upset about the beer bottle that rolled out from under the seat when he braked for a stoplight on the way to a family breakfast. According to Debbie, she did not actually drink but only acted as a designated driver for the other kids riding with her. Would *his* father have believed this, Bob wondered? Would it have made a difference in *his* punishment? Following this incident, Bob had an argument with his 15-year-old son, Gene, who wanted a pair of tennis shoes that cost more than Bob's first car, which he had had to buy and maintain himself.

Later that night, Bob and his wife, Lynette, who had first met in high school, attended their 25th high school reunion. The first topic of conversation was, of course,

how different everyone looked or how similar. As old
friends began to talk, some startling contrasts were re-
vealed. They first discovered that many of their friends
had changed spouses or life partners since the 10th reunion
(some more than once). While discussing these marital
changes, most remarked that their own parents were cele-
brating 40 to 50 years of marriage. Bob wondered how
many of today's teenagers would make a similar observation at their 25th high school reunion.

As Bob and Lynette reminisced with their friends, they
realized that they had known many of them since elemen-
tary school and had grown up in the same neighborhoods
in many cases. Unlike Bob and Lynette, many of these
friends had moved away. Those who had stayed in town,
like Bob and Lynette, had moved from one house to another as they climbed the social and financial ladder.

Bob's friend, Steve, was still showing off the scar over
his eye, evidence of Bob's bone-crushing tackle during
what had been described to parents as a game of "touch
football." Bob remembered being chewed out at dinner
that night in front of the whole family because his mother
had thought it was "too violent."

Lynette found herself in a conversation about the pressures of being a wife, mother and wage earner. Most of
the women seemed to share her frustration, and they all
generally agreed that for their own mothers, life roles
seemed much more predictable and less confusing.

Later on Lynette spotted Candy, who had sat next to
her in algebra before disappearing for almost a year during which it was rumored that she had been pregnant. In
those days, sex before marriage was considered "bad" and
publicly unacceptable, and Lynette and her friends had
often worried about their "reputations." Now her friends
are advising her to consider putting Debbie on birth control pills since "all girls are doing it at an earlier age."

As they listened to the oldies being played by the band,
several members of their group laughed about how the
music that sounded so fun, yet harmless now, was perceived then as "corrupting noise." However, they agreed

that much of today's teen music really is dangerous and requires no talent. They felt certain that none of the musical stars of *their* generation were at risk for arrest on charges of violence, obscenity or cruelty to animals.

It was only after the reunion that Bob and Lynette realized that the world in which they grew up no longer existed and how very different is the world in which their kids are growing up. The contrast between the two worlds helped them to understand that the changes were gradual. They had never before realized just how different their kids' adolescent world is from their own.

Their experiences are not unique.

Society has changed dramatically from the time when most of today's parents were adolescents themselves. Parents need to understand that these changes have an equally dramatic effect on the issues and pressures that today's kids and parents face.

These changes did not occur overnight, and their impact on families actually makes sense when viewed in their historical perspective. An understanding of these changes is necessary if parents are to develop philosophies and principles of parenting appropriate for adolescents of today, not yesterday.

Institutions

Alterations In The Basic Fabric Of Our Society

In general, societal change is reflected in the structure and character of its institutions. At the same time, institutions tend to operate as a foundation for society's belief system. Even more importantly, institutions have historically supplied a sense of stability and order that directs and facilitates the parenting process. But, beginning in the 1960s, long-standing American institutions began to go through a process of rapid change.

It is not our purpose to discuss all the reasons mobilizing the dramatic changes that began in the '60s. It also is not within the scope of this book to make judgments about the positive or negative value of these changes. Obviously, changes rooted in this time period had and continue to have beneficial effects on society. At the same time, these changes have resulted in a variety of trends, beliefs and lifestyle changes that have made parenting much more difficult and confusing. The purpose of our discussion is to summarize and describe changes within the four basic institutions — government, education, religion and parents themselves — that have an impact on the parenting process.

Society began to take a new direction during the period that included the popularity of the Beatles, the Rolling Stones and other rock groups. Popular music became a major medium of expression for the American public's dramatic shift in attitude and philosophy. As reflected in the lyrics of numerous songs of the time, people began to vigorously pursue "peace, love and brotherhood" as major, articulated goals. Reinforced by a corresponding preoccupation with the use of drugs as pathways to those goals, a younger generation gradually became convinced that fun, pleasure and feeling good were the true objectives of living. Responsibility, self-discipline, achievement and morality were definitely "uncool."

Traditional authority, in the form of governmental and societal rules, was a major block to this quest for pleasure and enjoyment. In fact, according to the folklore of that time, government was oppressive and antagonistic. Police became "pigs," and authority was perceived as something that maintained order and control by stifling creativity and expression of feelings. Disenchantment with and distrust of authority were further encouraged by both the Vietnam War and Watergate. Through these two historical events, the country and its leaders were shown to be untrustworthy, deceptive and insensitive to the feelings and attitudes of young people especially.

As disillusionment with government increased, there came a similar lack of commitment to other traditional

American institutions: religion and education. Church attendance decreased and instead of developing belief in God as a higher power, rhetoric encouraged individuals to believe that they themselves were supreme. Individual rights, beliefs and feelings superceded traditional values or work ethics. In essence, *me* replaced *thee*.

Schools as constant, stable institutions were also challenged. They found themselves strangled by public pressure and legislation. A new emphasis on socialization and a lack of funds to pursue both new and traditional goals placed serious limitations on their ability to teach basic academic curricula. Open classrooms replaced walls and assigned seats while creativity programs replaced the three Rs. The concept of teaching basics got buried in social relevancy. In addition, a school's ability to teach values and discipline was diminished. Questioning of traditional values led to value-less education. Teachers and administrators began to feel they were in no-win situations where society continued to have ever-increasing expectations of them. At the same time they were becoming less able to function as educators due to their own internal struggles with issues of race, accountability and protection of children's rights. Schools' loss of power as agents of change continues today.

However, one of the most stable parenting institutions in the past has been that of parents themselves. Parents have always learned about parenting from their own experience with their parents. Parents tend to do with their kids what was done with them. If, for example, a child was taught by his parents to respect his elders, then this child's children were taught the same basic principle by that child when he became a parent. (It should be noted that this particular parenting strategy is responsible for passing on unhealthy as well as healthy parenting practices.)

Even so, the process of parents teaching their children what was taught to them has historically been effective. This process worked when societal change was gradual and the world and children in one generation were very similar to the world and children in the previous generation. This is no longer the case. Technological and societal changes are occurring so rapidly that the childhood of today's adolescents is very different from the experience of their parents' adolescence. Thus, parents who attempt to do with their children what was done with them find themselves at a loss. How many of today's parents can pass on to their kids their own skills for coping with sexuality, drugs and peer pressure? It's impossible considering the average age of drug use in the '60s was approximately 16 and the average age of first drug use now is 11. Similarly, kids are making decisions about sex much earlier now than did their parents 25 years ago. Twenty-five years ago, issues regarding sex were basically the same from generation to generation. Issues regarding casual adolescent drug use were virtually nonexistent.

In the past, not only were parents themselves viewed as institutions, but society as a whole tended to serve as parents to its children. Kids had multiple parents; not only a mother and father who parented them, but also neighbors who were more than willing to correct behavior. In addition to correcting behavior, neighbors would most likely report misbehavior to parents. Store proprietors, Sunday school leaders, teachers, coaches, etc. all were quite willing to set limits and correct negative behavior. Adults, in general, accepted some measure of responsibility for parenting children whether the children were their own or not. Today, when neighbors, other adults or even the police attempt to discipline a child, such intervention is often unwelcome and unappreciated. In fact, those adults may even run the risk of being sued by disgruntled parents who feel their and their children's rights have been violated and their security threatened.

This lack of shared responsibility in today's society is influenced by the fact that it is an increasingly mobile society. Most adults know only a few of their neighbors and thus have less investment in their neighbors' children. Neighborhood schools are things of the past and attempts by school officials to organize parent groups frequently meet with a lack of interest.

To make matters worse, parents, schools and churches, out of frustration at their inability to influence children positively, often take turns blaming each other. Parents blame schools, schools blame parents, churches blame society, but no one group seems either able or willing to take full responsibility or to deal with the problems.

Media Influence

The net effect of these societal changes upon traditional institutions seems to be a subtle weakening of their ability to provide consistent values and behavioral guidelines for both children and adults. As the strength of these institutions has diminished, a new type of institution has arisen during the last three decades as a substitute. This new institution might be referred to as the electronic media, which includes television, movies and the music industry.

The electronic media embraces the pleasure principle of the '60s like a long-lost relative. Market share, album sales and Nielsen ratings are more important than the passing on of values, morals and education. Because the electronic media is made up largely of companies whose goal is profit, the emphasis of the electronic media is on fun and entertainment, not the teaching of mature values and behavior. If various consumer groups become concerned and attempt to put limits on negative messages conveyed by the media, the media typically responds that someone's freedom of speech or expression is being violated.

Research has shown that by age 18, an adolescent has viewed over 350,000 commercials on television. Approximately 70,000 of these commercials are related to drugs of some kind. Prevailing messages are "fix it now," "pain is bad," "you should feel no pain" and "if you are hurting, a chemical is your fix." All solutions provided by commercials for problems and pain come from outside an individual, because, of course, they can't sell you what you already have. There are no commercials suggesting the use of problem-solving, self-discipline or social support as solutions to pain.

While many 30-second commercials are detrimental in this way, it is those 30-minute commercials for the pleasure principle attitude toward life, commonly known as situation comedies, that may be the most destructive. In the early days of television when social values were more conservative and deviation from them less acceptable, sitcoms passed on such messages as "parents know best," "crime does not pay," and "success comes from hard work." Too many times, in a reflection of what *is* rather than what *should be,* today's messages seem "money and power buy happiness," "success comes from luck or connections," and "greed is good."

Furthermore, the lyrics of many of today's most popular rock songs horrify average parents, but receive little negative notice from teenagers who are inundated with such music. Unstable institutions rarely provide heroes and models for kids, but the media does. It is often rock stars who become higher powers and are worshipped by kids, as aptly demonstrated by this letter from an adolescent who wrote a local newspaper in response to that newspaper's review of a well-known rock band's concert. It reads as follows:

> "The concert was more than I could have hoped for
> . . . One cannot explain the feelings/emotions their music
> evokes. (Even if the decibels do warp one's hearing for a
> day or two.) This type of music (heavy metal) is not just
> an act. It is a way of life — even for a conservatively
> dressed middle-class girl like I am."

Other "higher powers" provided by the media include sports figures whose prominent athletic ability would appear to model self-discipline and hard work. However, such figures are often perceived by kids as symbols of wealth, power and fast living who seem to be puppets manipulated by the alcohol and tobacco industries who sponsor their sports events.

Clearly, parents cannot rely upon the electronic media to appropriately guide their kids. The electronic media is here to stay, however, and most people would agree that traditional institutions cannot be counted on to provide the consistent structure and type of foundation possible in previous generations. Today's society, while providing more individual freedom of thought and action, requires more individual strength and effort for effective coping. Parents need to assume primary responsibility for providing a system of guidelines, limits and values to guide the mature development of their children. That is the purpose of this book.

The Sexual Revolution

"What's Love Got To Do With It?"

After a light day in the office Ruth leaves for home an hour early, hoping to spend some extra time with her 14-year-old daughter, Mary. She feels that her daughter needs her more than ever now, since Mary is well into puberty and seems to be interested in boys. Ruth worries about having to allow Mary to date in a couple of years and at that time, Ruth plans to talk with her about sex.

As Ruth pulls into the drive, she notices a strange mini-bike on the porch. Upon entering the house, she encounters Mary with an unfamiliar zit-faced boy on the couch groping and petting in mutual exploration of each other's sexual anatomy. A startled Mary grabs her shirt and bra and runs into her room. The boy is speechless as he stumbles out the door and exits onto his two-wheeled studmachine.

When Ruth shares her shock, disappointment and anger with her daughter, she is attacked for invading Mary's privacy by having the gall to come home unexpectedly. As the conversation progresses, Mary finally begins to cry and explains to her mother that this boy is very popular. Mary, too, wants to be popular, and to do this, she must have a popular boyfriend. Mary further reasons that all popular girls "do it" with their boyfriends, and if she is not willing to get involved sexually, she will be seen as a nerd and have no friends, an idea that terrifies her.

Ruth is taken totally by surprise, not only by Mary's behavior, but by her attitude toward sex.

Ruth, welcome to the '90s!

Dramatic shifts in how society expresses sexuality began in the '60s. Along with peace and brotherhood, the Beatles informed us that *All You Need Is Love*. But in this generation, love came to be associated not so much with caring, giving and commitment, but rather with sexual pleasure. This may very well have resulted from the previous generation's search for a means of dealing with anxiety created by the turbulent times. What feels good in terms of physical pleasure is certainly much easier to define and obtain than is the quest for intimacy and spirituality. Everyone's body is programmed for physical pleasure, but not everyone has the personal skills and potential to guarantee an emotionally intimate and gratifying relationship.

Sex used to be governed by a variety of publicly held social rules such as "Sex before marriage is wrong." These rules were intended to make sex special, a thing of intimacy. With the permissiveness of the '60s, sex became associated with fun and liking, rather than intimacy and love. Sex was just another way the "me generation" indulged itself. It was one of the most accessible quick fixes around, just another form of "Satisfaction," as the Rolling Stones sang in 1966. Sex became a comparatively casual, commonplace topic of discussion. Books and magazines very openly described the latest techniques and mechanics necessary to heighten sexual pleasure. Individuals of all generations suddenly became self-conscious as they attempted to rate the quality and frequency of their own sexual performance. Marriages were dissolved, not because of neglect, cruelty, or irreconcilable differences, but due to sexual incompatibility.

The sexual revolution permeated society. It is difficult to find an area where its effect is not felt. Our preoccupation with and acceptance of open sexuality is, again, best reflected in the media. A common thread in many situation comedies, television dramas, movies and best sellers since the sexual revolution has been a preoccupation with superficial sexual relating, promiscuity and sex as a competitive sport.

The front page of any newspaper almost always discusses the latest development regarding sexually transmitted diseases, teenage pregnancy or sex education in schools. In any analysis of politicians and political races, media focus is frequently on candidates' personal lives, especially their sexuality, rather than the pertinent issues in each candidate's political platform.

This public preoccupation with sex has had a tremendous effect on teen culture. Whereas a few years ago an individual's first experience with sexual intercourse was publicly associated with marriage, the average age of first sexual intercourse is now 15. Teen music is filled with direct and graphic sexual references.

Sex education in school tends to focus not upon values, but avoiding negative consequences. This may result from the public's increasing distrust of school systems' abilities to function as parental substitutes and to impart values. Mirroring adult culture, teens tend to view sex not only as a fun fix, but as a symbol of power and status.

Unfortunately, this superficial attitude toward sex has the same result in the teen culture as it does in adult counterparts. While teens may attempt to cope with their insecurity by becoming sexually active, they often feel empty, alone and insecure instead. In addition, the increasing incidence of sexually transmitted disease is an area of much concern. New strains of herpes, gonorrhea and syphilis are being discovered, not to mention the deadly devastation and fear aroused by AIDS. At some level, most teens realize that sex does not lead to confidence and self-esteem, but too often they lack the knowledge, skill and alternatives necessary to travel the road to real happiness and contentment.

The Drug Revolution

Better Living Through Chemistry?

Gary is feeling frustrated. Jason, his 16-year-old son, was supposed to be home at 11:30 p.m. It is now 12:10 a.m. Gary had felt somewhat uncomfortable earlier this evening because he did not like the looks of the friend who picked Jason up. Gary had never seen this boy before and the name was unfamiliar. Jason said he was not sure of the boy's last name but assured his dad that he was an "okay dude." Jason said they were just going out to do "some stuff and ride around" but now Gary wishes he had asked more questions.

Jason finally sails in an hour late and makes a beeline for his room. Gary intercepts him on the stairs, demanding to know why he is late. Gary notices Jason will not make eye contact and that he seems a little wobbly. After an angry confrontation, Jason admits that he "just had a couple of beers." Gary sends him to bed, saying they will talk about it in the morning.

Inwardly Gary is somewhat relieved thinking, "Wow, I was really worried that Jason was getting into drugs. I am so glad it's only beer." Gary knows he probably should ground Jason, but he is thinking back to his own teenage days when he did the same thing and thinks, "I turned out okay, didn't I?" But then Gary also remembers that his dad did ground him for what seemed like forever, and it was quite a while before he was willing to once again risk his freedom for a "buzz." Just because Gary understands that it's normal for Jason to want to try drinking, as he did, doesn't mean that he has to accept or ignore the behavior. His father didn't and maybe that's why he turned out okay.

Gary has no idea of the difference between the adolescent drug culture of the '90s and the atmosphere of the '60s in which he grew up. In addition, he has absolutely no understanding of the difference in drug availability today or even how different drugs are today from the ones he knew so well 25 years ago.

Modern American society is the most drug-abusive society in the history of the world. The illegal drug business constitutes one of the largest "corporations" of any type operating in the country today and represents profits equaling the entire economy of many other countries. Due to the incredible profits available in illegal drugs, the most sophisticated research and business principles are being applied to the manufacture and sale of illegal drugs. In addition, recent statistics indicate that the drug problem in our society is responsible, directly or indirectly, for a large percentage of crimes committed today.

How has society changed so drastically in the last 25 years? The answer is complicated. Drug abuse has been a problem for thousands of years. Drug use existed before the '60s but never before received mainstream social acceptance or encouragement. With the cultural revolution that started in the '60s, drug use emerged as an acceptable behavior. Never before had society not only said drugs were okay, but encouraged individuals to experiment and to "turn on, tune in, drop out" as Harvard professor Timothy Leary suggested. Drug use was touted as a road to higher consciousness and a path to self-actualization and enlightenment. Since authority was not to be trusted, any warnings or laws about drug use were seen as oppressive tools of discredited institutions and thus discounted.

Societal attitudes tolerating, even favoring, drug use, and distrust of authority and institutions set the stage in 1970 for a major piece of legislation that had a tremendously destructive impact on adolescents: the legal age for purchasing alcohol was reduced from 21 to 18.

When the majority of today's parents were growing up, the drinking age was 21. On a practical level, this meant that 17- and 18-year-olds could buy alcohol using fake IDs. They, in turn, would sell to 15- and 16-year-olds. When the drinking age was lowered from 21 to 18, this same process continued. However, 15- and 16-year-olds then used fake IDs to pass for 18 and buy alcohol. They, in turn, would sell it to the 12-, 13- and 14-year-olds. Thus societal attitudes and legislation conspired to lower the age at which kids functionally had more ready access to alcohol. Age of initial access and experimentation with alcohol is a terribly important factor. The younger children are when experimentation with alcohol and other drugs begins, the more devastating the destructive impact on their intellectual, social, emotional and neurological maturation. At younger ages, fewer healthy behavioral controls are developed, and the mixture of this immaturity with mind-altering substances is a dangerous combination.

Today the average age for first-time experience with alcohol is 11 years old for boys and 11 and a half years old for girls. Alcohol is still not viewed as a drug by many adults and this attitude is picked up by children. Many adolescents experiment with alcohol in the form of wine coolers, which seem like soft drinks to them. After any ingestion of alcohol, judgment is impaired, inhibitions are released and the likelihood of experimentation with other drugs is increased. Healthy psychological maturation depends on developing children's ability to accurately interpret reality. All of the drugs commonly used by adolescents, including alcohol, are psychoactive and thus distort reality. Adolescent treatment centers make the common observation that maturation stops when drug use starts. The increasingly younger ages at which adolescents begin to experiment with psychoactive drugs has led to an increasingly out of control and destructive teenage subculture.

The media has both reflected and stimulated society's preoccupation with chemical fixes for all problems. During the 1960s, the slogan "Better Living Through Chemistry" was taken quite seriously. Society became obsessed with a bigger or better pill to cure all ills and remove all pain. The phrases "Excedrin headache" and "taking a powder" came to reflect society's acceptance of drug use as a response to normal situational stress. The subtle value underlying these commercials is troubling. They imply that pain is bad and should be avoided at all costs.

This concept in commercial advertising also gave rise to Olympic competition between pill manufacturers as to who could manufacture the biggest pill, the message being that if 300 mg was good, then 500 mg must be better. In addition, the media was quite effective at continuing the myth that alcohol is not a drug. Since "hard" liquor is not allowed to be advertised on TV, and beer and wine are displayed everywhere on TV, the obvious conclusion to be drawn is that liquor is clearly different from beer and wine. However, the active ingredient is exactly the same in both substances and varies only in concentration. Society continues to maintain its denial that alcohol is a drug. However, alcohol continues to be the number-one drug of abuse among teenagers. It is also their number-one killer.

Another issue affecting today's parents as they deal with drug questions is the fact that they grew up with a very liberal, yet less-educated perspective on the drug culture. Research on alcohol and marijuana in the last 20 years has provided a much better understanding of the danger and destructive impact of these drugs. Many parents raised in the '60s don't consider alcohol a drug, and many don't even consider beer an alcoholic beverage. In addition, marijuana was thought to be harmless, less dangerous than alcohol. NORML, the National Organization for the Reform of Marijuana Laws, organized in the '60s, still campaigns for the legalization of marijuana. We now know that alcohol is most definitely a drug and that marijuana, which today is 10 to 20 times more potent that it was in the '60s, is more destructive than ever imagined.

Most parents today are completely out of touch with the drug-using adolescent subculture. They measure and evaluate adolescent drug use with an out-of-date yardstick based on inadequate information and an incomplete understanding of today's teenagers and the world in which they live.

The Changing Family

"Ward, Where Is The Beaver?"

Will is a typical teenager of the '90s. He lives with his mother and stepfather. His parents divorced eight years

ago when Will was six. His mother remarried four years
ago. He has a 12-year-old sister and a half-brother who is
almost three. His father, who lives out of town, remarried
shortly after the divorce and has two children with Will's
stepmother.

Will used to visit his father fairly regularly and called
weekly. Now visits have dropped off, and his dad does not
seem to call as often as he invests his efforts in his new
family. Will's mother and stepfather both work so Will is
frequently expected to supervise his younger siblings.

Change in the structure of American family in the last
30 years has had a tremendous impact on society and
vice versa. Those with excellent memories can remember
what is still considered the traditional American family: a
mother, a father and several children, with one parent
working to provide financial support and the other parent
at home caring for the kids. Of course, both parents had
been married only to each other. This traditional family
is a rarity today. Blended families are increasingly accepted as the statistical norm. In addition, in the majority of
American families, both parents work. Traditional families unaffected by divorce and with only one parent working now represent fewer than 10 percent of American
families. The more common family situations in America
today are single parent families, blended families and
families with both parents working.

Single Parent Families

Increasingly, parenting without partners is posing a new
set of challenges to those trying to raise well-adjusted
kids in a poorly adjusted society. Whether parents are
single as a result of death, divorce or planned decision-
making, single parents face an exhausting number of demands on their time and emotions. It is difficult to provide
structure and supervision because the demands of working environments can seldom be adjusted easily around
the needs of children. Quality care for preschool children
is difficult to find. School-age children frequently come

home to empty houses. And the combination of pent-up energy from the school day and lack of adult supervision can easily lead to negative peer-related activities.

Single parents, usually mothers, frequently feel a lack of emotional and physical support for their efforts, which leads to significant feelings of frustration and helplessness. Single parents often experience guilt over their inability to provide sufficient time and energy to parenting, yet also feel overwhelmed by the demands of full-time jobs and full-time families.

Single parents frequently feel vulnerable and alone emotionally and may seek to have their emotional needs met by their children rather than adult relationships. Kids may feel pressured to grow up too quickly and to deal with their parents on a level for which they are not ready developmentally. These children often have difficulty accepting discipline and limits from parents who treat them more as peers than as developing children.

Single parents are frequently lonely and characterized by feelings of alienation, isolation and powerlessness. Demands made by an increasingly complex and alienated society are difficult for single adults, much less single parents. Increasingly creative measures are needed to maintain support and structure for parents and children alike.

Blended Families

Many families today need scorecards to keep track of biological parents, stepparents, natural brothers and sisters, half brothers and sisters, and stepbrothers and sisters. It's difficult to keep relationships straight, much less maintain consistency in family structure, values development and discipline. It is easy to see the tremendous conflicts that can arise from the combination of blended relationships and unresolved emotional conflict from original family breakups. Stepparents frequently feel ineffective, frustrated and unappreciated by children of their new partners. They are frequently met with cries of, "He's not my father," or "She's not my mother and she can't tell me what to do." In blended families, deciding who or what combination of parents will provide discipline and structure is a frequent source of conflict between adults and children. Limit-setting and discipline become battlegrounds which drive wedges into new marital relationships, thus providing even less stability for children.

While it is difficult to provide consistent discipline in blended families, it is almost impossible for parents to maintain any consistency at all when visits to noncustodial parents are added. It would be great if divorced parents could maintain mature working relationships for the benefit of their children. However, this is the exception, not the rule. When differences between adults are severe enough to lead to divorce, it is unlikely that these same parents will agree in consistent fashion on how their kids should be raised within different households. In addition, parents are frequently afraid that children will choose to live with noncustodial parents, to the point of affecting limit-setting and structure within families.

When both adults in new marriages have biological children, differential treatment of biological children versus stepchildren becomes a difficult area of discussion. Marrying adults tend to expect, unrealistically, that biological and nonbiological children will be treated identically and completely fairly and tend to ignore the historical bond that distinguishes biological relationships. It's easy for adults to recognize they are more tolerant of their own kids' transgressions than they are of their neighbors' kids, but they tend to overlook this when marriage between these neighbors enters the picture. Children frequently feel stuck in the middle of adult conflict and look for security that parents have been unable to give themselves, much less their children. In addition, parents frequently expect their biological children to "love" stepparents when this is an inappropriate expectation for children who have no real history with this new adult. Just because Mom or Dad loves this new partner doesn't mean their children automatically will.

A workable marriage requires effort and has its difficult moments. When multiple members are added, each with their own set of needs and maturity levels, a desire for professional referees is frequently felt.

Two-Career Families

Changing roles for men and women in society have an enormous impact on family units. Tremendous upheaval in the traditionally accepted male and female roles has left many adults feeling confused and isolated in the feelings they bring to the role of mother or father. In the past, questions about who worked, who disciplined and who nurtured were easily answered. This is no longer the case as more and more women enter the workplace, pursuing careers and providing that increasingly important second paycheck. Parental guilt is at an all-time high as parents feel a tremendous desire to be involved in their children's lives, yet find it difficult to make time for their children. There are books on the "one-minute mother" and the "one minute father," and it is easy for parents to feel that they are not doing it right if they don't feel fulfilled as parents with 30 seconds of quality time per day, per child.

When both parents work, it is difficult to decide who will take responsibility for handling daily problems associated with raising kids. Who leaves the office when the school calls and says a child is sick and needs to be picked up? And while it is certainly true that both Mom and Dad can have a 40-hour work week, studies indicate that women continue to shoulder more of the caretaking responsibility than do men.

And what has happened to weekends? In the past, weekends were seen as time to catch up on family leisure-time activities. Now weekends are used to catch up on chores not addressed during the work week. Time for family bonding becomes less and less available. Family togetherness is characterized less by emotional bonding and more by increased responsibility for getting the chores done.

The three family types described above are more and more the most common experiences for children and adults in society today. These family situations represent difficult challenges to the traditional concepts of parenting and family cohesiveness, especially when families experience a combination of situations.

An increase in the number of families where both parents work has led to at least one common major change in the parenting of children. More often, children are being raised from infancy in daycare settings by "professional parents." This can encourage children to shift their approval-seeking from adults (parents) to their peers at an earlier age. When at least one parent spends time during the day caretaking, children do not become excessively peer-oriented in their approval seeking until the early school years. Thus children are exposed to parental values for a longer, more intense duration. Hopefully, parental values reflect more maturity, morality and responsibility than do the values of the average preschool peer.

In addition, the amount of exposure children have to adults and mature adult values is a direct function of how many kids are in a family. In any of the families described above, with from one to four involved parents and an average of two to four children, maximum exposure to parental values is available. Typical "preschool families" average 10 to 15 children. Thus, the amount of parental or adult exposure available to kids in preschool settings is diminished. Children today receive less consistent structure than ever before.

The fast pace encountered by most working parents leaves little time for traditional parent-child interaction. At the end of a long workday, both parents come home exhausted, with little energy left over for kids. So there is little opportunity for quality emotional contact, structure or nurturance. What happened to family dinners? Fast food has taken control of nutrition in many homes today.

An unfortunate byproduct of these changes in family structure, cohesiveness and strength of parental unity has been an increasing focus on superficial relating. An emphasis on deep-seated values based on commitment and belief is missing, as is the focus on what is right as opposed to what is comfortable.

This increasing focus on superficiality in relationships, especially in relationships between parents and children, has raised materialism to an art form. Today kids and adults alike are preoccupied with materialistic gains. Unfortunately, parents may see adolescent preoccupation with possessions as an opportunity to provide nurturant substitutes in the form of gifts. This encourages and enhances the hedonistic pursuit of pleasure by adolescents.

Many parents feel their adolescents are learning responsibility and the value of a dollar because they have part-time jobs. However, now more than ever, kids' part-time job earnings purchase only luxuries and "wants" as opposed to contributing to family income, household necessities or savings. These children are being trained in premature affluence. These same children may be unprepared to deal with the responsibilities of living in the adult world when their only interaction with earning money has been to use it for luxuries.

Instilling values in kids is time-consuming, laborious and frequently unrewarding on an immediate basis. However, families are the primary arena in which children learn basic values.

Teaching values effectively is done in families through children's observation of how parents live their lives and manage their responsibilities, each other and themselves.

The increasing loss of structure in today's families creates dangerous obstacles that potentially can hamper children's abilities to learn the basic traditional values necessary to the maturity process.

4

Parenting Myths

Ray Mendez is frustrated. He has been married to Mark's mother Carla for almost a year and he is still having difficulty establishing an appropriate relationship with Mark. Mark is 11 and still angry about his parents' divorce. He is rude to his stepfather, ignores him and often asks his mother, in front of Ray, when they are going to get divorced. Just this evening, Mr. Mendez told Mark to move his bicycle and skateboard off the steps where he had left them the night before. Mark told him he did not feel like it. When told he could expect a consequence for his refusal to mind, Mark looked squarely at his stepfather and stated, "You can't tell me what to do. You're not my real dad."

Mrs. Stone has just said no to a request by her daughter Rachel to stay out later than usual after a basketball game on a school night. This has resulted in Rachel arguing, yelling at her mother and slamming doors. Mrs. Stone feels frustrated, confused, angry, guilty and totally out of control. She has no idea what to say to her daughter next or how to effectively deal with the situation.

Mr. Mendez and Mrs. Stone are not alone. When parents are confronted with these and other common adolescent parenting situations, they typically respond with information and skill from four basic areas.

Probably the primary source of information for parents is their own upbringing. Parents look to their own parents and the way they were raised as a model for raising their own kids. Generally speaking, information from this source probably is valid and effective in many situations. After all, these same techniques were responsible for guiding today's parents to the mature, independent level of functioning that prompted them to buy this book. However, information from this source does not take into account the dramatic societal changes that have occurred over the last 25 years. Another problem is that many parents remember their own parents' inadequacies and deficiencies and may be reluctant to use them as models.

Just as parents look to their own parents as a guide to the parenting process, they also draw from beliefs, attitudes and ideals that existed during their own childhood and adolescence. Many of today's parents grew up in the turbulent '60s, which emphasized distrust of institutions, authority and tradition. During this period society gave rise to a cult of narcissism, often referred to as the "Me Generation." The Me Generation tended to discount the impact of institutions and looked instead to individual needs, feelings and heroes to determine appropriate values and directions.

Ideal life in the '60s advocated pleasure, peace and happiness while avoiding situations involving worry or responsibility. Music, folklore and prevailing philosophies of the time encouraged individuals to "do their own thing," "find themselves," and "go with their own feelings" to places that were "far out" and "groovy."

So parents who were adolescents in the '60s may lean toward a permissive, *laissez-faire* style of parenting. They tend to avoid conflict, have difficulty taking a stand and can easily be influenced by their own peers. Traces of '60s philosophy are present in parents who are naive and idealistic, and they lack trust in their own judgment. These parents often are overly concerned with their children's feelings of immediate happiness and pleasure rather than emphasizing the development of values and true living skills.

Confusing Messages

Other sources of information available to today's parents are the media and the current social climate. We've already looked at these messages, which emphasize materialism, quick fixes, promiscuous sexuality and self-indulgence. Children, especially adolescents, are being given more and more access to information and experience formerly reserved for adults. Yet parents receive conflicting messages about how to intervene and establish some sense of control over their children's exposure to such situations.

Given the confusing messages from society as well as their own experience, parents often resort to magazines and books on parenting as a final source of information. Unfortunately, most parenting books stimulate parents to feel even more confused, misguided and uncertain than before. While such books can be loaded with advice, they can and do contradict each other. For example, various child care experts at one time or another have advised parents to: set limits, be permissive, love and accept their kid's behavior regardless of how destructive it is, be friends with their child, be responsible for their child's behavior, not be responsible for their child's behavior, realize that negative behavior is caused by learning disabilities, understand that problems are caused by low self-esteem and view drug use as a relatively harmless part of the passage from childhood to adulthood.

Faced with such conflicting messages, it is no wonder parents feel confused and insecure when they encounter relatively normal crises and problems of adolescence. The misinformation can be sorted into four basic myths about parenting. To develop healthy, effective approaches to today's adolescents, each parent must work hard to identify and overcome these false assumptions.

Myth #1: Adolescents Are Miniature Adults

The miniature adult theory says adolescents are not really children but are smaller versions of adults. As such, it is assumed they possess levels of judgment, morality and self-esteem only slightly below an adult level. The miniature adult theory very clearly has strong roots in the '60s because it was during that time that youth came to believe they were being discriminated against since they were just as smart as their parents and deserved the same freedom and privileges as those who were much older and more experienced. Consistent with this belief, many judged adolescents to be "young adults" possessing innate guides to development. Adolescents were viewed as completely able to choose their own values and make appropriate decisions.

The net result of this thinking is the belief that adolescent children can think, feel and make decisions at the same level as their parents. When parents assume their adolescent children think like adults, they use adult techniques to try to influence their behavior. Rather than applying the law of natural consequences, parents adhering to the miniature adult theory tend to react with facts, explanations, guilt trips and scare tactics. Parents reason that if these techniques are effective on themselves, they will surely work on their "young adults."

Following this assumption, Mrs. Stone would explain to Rachel that the no was in Rachel's best interests. Mrs. Stone would attempt to counter all of Rachel's irrational objections with reason, only to end up feeling exasperated and angry when Rachel still fails to agree with and accept the limit. Mr. Mendez would sit down with Mark and explain that as a stepfather, he doesn't want to replace Mark's natural father. When this rational explanation fails to change Mark's defiant, manipulative attitude toward him, Mr. Mendez feels even more hurt and frustrated.

School systems adhere to the miniature adult theory. Adolescent and pre-adolescent children are "educated" about the hazards and pitfalls of sex and drugs with facts and information about long-term consequences. The assumption is that this information will influence them to make better decisions. Unfortunately, too many parents and educators fail to realize that adolescents are not fully rational in their thinking and perceptions.

Belief in the miniature adult theory is also very evident in much of the advice given to parents by mental health professionals. For example, a parent asked a newspaper columnist, "What can I do about my 13-year-old daughter who smokes?"

The child care expert answered: "There is no reason to allow your child to smoke in your own home. Why not try calling the American Cancer Society for material you can share? And you might ask the school counselor for what the school is doing."

In our opinion, this is naive advice. Every 13-year-old child already knows that cigarette smoking is harmful, yet many adolescents obviously choose to ignore that fact and typically smoke because they want to feel more independent and grown up. More facts and information will not solve the problem.

In another example from the same article, a parent asked, "What is the right age for wearing makeup? My 10-year-old daughter wants to."

The answer given by the expert was: "Don't get involved in the age game. My belief is that you worry about your child's health, safety and ability to function in a positive way. The makeup is not a problem unless she is so obsessed with it that it detracts from school work. Then it is unhealthy and you can explain that to her."

Apparently this expert thinks a 10-year-old should be able to make her own decision about makeup. Should parents take similar stances concerning drug use, sex or negative peers? After all, parents are advised to worry only if the problem "detracts from school work." This child is attempting to act like an adult prematurely and probably views makeup as a way of making herself more attractive and acceptable to her peer group. But parents — not children — should make decisions about when children are ready to assume the responsibilities and privileges of maturity, such as wearing makeup.

When parents, educators and mental health professionals consciously or unconsciously adhere to the miniature adult theory, they are forgetting that adolescence is a stage of *childhood*. Children cannot be expected to think, feel, moralize and reason on adult levels.

Myth #2: It's Just a Stage

The stage theory implies that such typical adolescent behavior as moodiness, rebelliousness, preoccupation with peer acceptance and alcohol/drug use is simply a phase that will disappear if ignored. Belief in the stage theory appears, superficially at least, to be based upon valid understanding of psychology and adolescence as a stage of development. It is true that adolescents go through a period of separation, independence and even rebelliousness as a normal part of their growing up and maturation process. Problems occur when parents and child-care experts assume that, because rebellious behavior and premature striving for independence are normal, parents should not intervene or take a stand when such behavior is exhibited. Parents may be led to believe that since such behavior is normal, it will go away or resolve itself in time with no permanent or damaging effects to individuals or families. Adolescents will simply "grow out of it." Parents are therefore encouraged to wish, hope, pray and be patient during this 10-year period called adolescence.

This attitude is particularly dangerous when applied to the issue of alcohol and other drug use among adolescents. Frankly, given the epidemic levels of alcohol and other drug abuse among adolescents today, it is appalling that parents are encouraged to take anything but a firm, strong stand against such behavior. In fact, not addressing early adolescent experimentation with alcohol and other drugs would seem to foster and perpetuate the development of a potentially severe and life-threatening problem. Similarly lying, stealing, smoking, reckless driving and skipping school are all fairly typical adolescent behaviors. But these behaviors will most likely continue or get worse, not disappear, if they are not met by parental intervention.

Operating under the asumptions of the stage theory, Mrs. Stone simply needs to try harder to be patient and understanding with Rachel and pray for the day when Rachel's arguing and disrespect will magically cease. She might also attempt to compromise with Rachel to make life easier until the stage passes. Mr. Mendez would simply endure Mark's verbal abuse and disrespect, thinking that in a few years Mark will naturally come to respect and appreciate his stepfather.

While it is true that adolescence is a stage of growth and development, the fact that it is a normal stage does not mean that parents do not need to intervene and provide guidance. Our belief is to the contrary. Adolescents do not possess the ability to raise themselves. They very much need direction, guidance and intervention from parents, who hopefully know more about responsible living.

Myth #3: Parents Control Their Children's Behavior

While '60s parents were learning to be more permissive in their approach to parenting, they unfortunately were also learning to feel totally responsible for their children's actions. An extreme example is childhood autism, now understood as a severe neurological disorder, but then thought by experts to be caused by cold, distant parenting. Child care experts, espousing the beliefs of "humanism," blamed children's behavioral/emotional problems upon parents being overly rigid, controlling and not communicating appropriately with their children. According to that model, when children are unhappy or in trouble, it is always their parents' fault. When adolescents act up in class, skip school or do something inappropriate, who gets the phone call from the principal or the guidance counselor? Schools seem to assume that parents can magically control their children's behavior in the school setting.

Parents have the greatest difficulty dealing with their kids when they personalize their adolescents' behavior, that is, when parents take full responsibility for choices their children make and tie their self-esteem as parents and their worth as individuals to their adolescents' actions. Thus the parents of a drug-using teenager will say, "If Scott is using drugs, we are bad parents." Similarly the parents of an adolescent not doing her homework feel they must have done something wrong if their child is having academic problems. In fact, Scott is using drugs because he has chosen to do so. The same applies to teenagers who don't do their homework, teenagers who skip school, teenagers who are defiant and teenagers who are honor students, cheerleaders or athletic stars.

It is important for parents to realize that responsibility for their children does not make them responsible for their children's choices.

Parents are responsible for instilling values, setting rules and limits, and providing positive and negative consequences for the choices their children make in response to these rules and limits.

If a parent's self-esteem is tied too closely to a child's behavior, that parent will be unable to respond to destructive behavior in an effective manner due to fear, guilt, anger or frustration. In fact, it is probably this tendency toward personalization of adolescent behavior that is the major cause for what is often referred to as "parental denial."

Parents in denial often unconsciously block awareness of destructive or negative behavior demonstrated by their adolescent. A primary motive for this unconscious inability to see problem behavior is that realization of their children's problems causes guilt, shame and frustration because parents assume they are responsible, not their children.

When Mrs. Stone accepts this false assumption in dealing with Rachel, she actually thinks it is her fault that Rachel is argumentative. However, because this belief makes Mrs. Stone feel guilty and like a failure as a parent, she avoids these unpleasant feelings by rationalizing that the limit is too strict. She then relaxes the limit, gives Rachel her way and temporarily avoids discomfort about her parenting. Similarly, Mr. Mendez feels guilty and inadequate because Mark has not accepted him as a stepfather and an authority figure. Mr. Mendez therefore defers all decision-making to his wife, Mark's mother, hoping that Mark will no longer perceive him as acting as if he's trying to replace Mark's natural father.

It is critical that adolescents accept responsibility for their own behavior if they are to become responsible adults. Parents foster irresponsibility in their children by feeling too responsible for the choices their children make instead of taking responsibility for setting values and limits and providing consequences for violating these standards. For adolescents to accept responsibility for their choices and develop a sense of responsibility as individuals, parents must attain a certain level of detachment.

Detachment, in a psychological sense, refers to the process of achieving emotional distance, objectivity and perspective in close, caring relationships. Detachment is not rejection, hate or insensitivity. In fact, detachment is a necessary ingredient in loving parent/adolescent relationships. It allows adolescents to become independent and responsible. When parents are too close and involved with their adolescents on an emotional level, they tend to lose their objectivity and their ability to separate their needs from their adolescents' wants. Similarly, overly attached parents have difficulty distinguishing between what is best for their adolescents and what feels comfortable to them as parents. Detachment is necessary for parents to effectively set and enforce limits, since making rules and applying consequences are particularly unpleasant, yet extremely important tasks for parents.

Closely related to the belief that parents are responsible for adolescent behavior is the belief that parents are also in control of adolescent behavior. Parents have a variety of beliefs about their power over their children's behavior that lead them to feel guilty and frustrated when their children don't act the way they expect. In particular, overly aggressive and authoritarian parents tend to believe their children should be under their control. When adolescents assert their beliefs and personalities, these parents respond with exasperated, inappropriate attempts to control them.

In Rachel's case, Mrs. Stone simply says, "I told you not to argue or yell at me again." She then goes ahead and gives Rachel her way and is surprised when Rachel argues again the next time she is told no. Mr. Mendez decides to bear down and show Mark that he is, in fact, a legitimate authority figure in the home. Mr. Mendez then reverts to spanking and severe grounding and threatens to send Mark to live with his "real" father in his unrealistic bid to gain Mark's acceptance of him as an authority figure.

This prevalent mistaken belief is reflected in the much-used parental injunction, "You will do as I tell you to do." *Wrong*. Kids will do exactly what they choose to do. Granted, they will frequently choose to do what their parents tell them to do, but the choice is an active one. Their behavior is not directly controlled by parental statements. Until adolescent behavior is internally controlled by values and beliefs, their behavioral choices will, most likely, reflect awareness of the consequences for each of those choices. To the old saying, "You can lead a horse to water, but you can't make him drink" must be added, "But if you make him thirsty enough, he just might choose to drink on his own."

How many times have parents felt like that fellow leading the horse to water and being frustrated by not being able to make him drink? Parents need to let children know the water (limit or rule) is there, make them thirsty (motivate by awareness of positive and negative consequences), and focus on willingness instead of excuses.

This approach is a direct representation of the real world with which adolescents will have to deal when assuming adult responsibilities. Parents do their children a disservice by preparing them for an unrealistic world. The adult world is based on choices and consequences. Mature parents and adults eventually learn that healthy choices result in positive consequences. Unhealthy choices result in negative consequences. Adolescents need to learn this to function effectively as adults.

Rules and limits (set by parents) don't control (children's) behavior. If that were true, every car on the highway would go 55 m.p.h. because that is the speed limit.

All rules and limits are merely stated standards about which choices must be made by individuals.

All people, children and adults alike, make choices based either on internal values, expected consequences or both. Children frequently make poor, immature choices because they are immaturely developed human beings. They are not finished, even though they may look completely formed.

Children frequently demand freedom, with the mistaken belief that freedom means no restrictions. A mature definition of freedom is the awareness of one's ability to choose. Children are constantly making choices. It is probably this very fact that is so terrifying to parents that they try to deal with their anxiety by using the authoritarian, "You will do as I say." Choicemaking is a healthy, powerful, self-affirming process. Awareness of the ability to make choices is a key ingredient in self-esteem and self-confidence.

Myth #4: Problems And Unhappiness Are Bad

The belief that problems are bad and that individuals should never have to experience uncomfortable feelings also seems to have been generated by the self-indulgent attitude of the '60s. A reformulated definition of personal problems stated that if an individual experiences pain, then something is clearly wrong. According to this very destructive redefinition, someone or something external is usually responsible. The too-common conclusion is that people in pain are being mistreated or getting a raw deal. Characteristically, the Me Generation approach to many problems was to find whoever or whatever was to blame and change them or it. Personal responsibility was discounted and the search for external perpetrators began. Refusing to accept responsibility for one's life, blaming the environment or others, and a strong sense of entitlement are key features of the Me Generation. These concepts and beliefs provide superficial psychological salve to the pain of experiencing problems. However, superficial relief provided by blaming others became the foundation for an epidemic of low self-esteem because those who do not take responsibility for their problems can never take credit for their successes.

Psychological theories at that time reflected the prevailing climate and tended to foster "victimization of the individual." Parents were chastised for being insensitive and not using enough positive reinforcement. Teachers and school officials were counseled to avoid any type of discipline that caused discomfort and focus instead only upon the positive characteristics of students. While positive reinforcement is extremely important, it cannot completely replace discipline and consequences. Unfortunately, both parents and teachers tended to go too far and interpret much of this advice as "make children happy at all costs."

Certainly the belief that everyone should always be happy is very much reinforced by messages from society and the media. Given this background, it is not surprising that adolescents attempt to avoid pain and emotional discomfort at all costs.

Too often adolescents identify pain as stemming directly from their problems. They therefore want to escape the trouble or have parents remove the problem for them. In many cases adolescents believe that happiness is a function of not having any problems. Obviously this is absurd. Problems are a normal part of life. Those not experiencing any problems whatsoever should check their pulse. Adolescents must learn that pain often comes not from the problem itself, but from the way they tend to deal with particular problems. Adolescents need to learn that while pain is normal, particular choices and approaches to problems can have an effect upon how pain is experienced. Adolescents need to know that their methods of coping with problems are their own responsibility and under their control.

In the case of Rachel, Mrs. Stone would be operating under the "problems are bad" myth if she changed her no to yes because she became worried that Rachel might be unhappy and suffer needlessly because of the limit. Mr. Mendez would buy his stepson a new skateboard, reasoning that Mark was experiencing undue pain due to the divorce of his natural parents. Adolescents who feel unpopular with their peers have a problem. However if they choose to use drugs, run away, join a negative peer group or drop out of school as a means of dealing with this problem, then they have a much more severe problem and will ultimately experience even more pain. Adolescents need to be taught that problems are normal, and that parents are not responsible for removing all problems and negative feelings from their children's lives. In fact, it is parental discipline that sets the stage upon which adolescents learn how to deal with pain in the form of frustration, disappointment and negative consequences. Learning to deal with these feelings and situations effectively helps adolescents to function in a more adult, real-world manner. Kids need to learn that they are frequently not victims of circumstances (which tends to excuse destructive choices and coping techniques) and learn to deal appropriately with problems.

Preparation For Decision-Making

It should be obvious from the preceding discussion that if parents adhere to these myths, they may unintentionally reinforce irresponsibility, dependence and immaturity. In-

stead we recommend a plan for good parenting that embraces the concept of approaching children in a manner
that prepares them to live independently in the adult
world. Therefore, during the adolescent years, adolescents
need to make significant progress in the areas of responsible decision-making, development of healthy value systems and the establishment of positive self-identities. Parents need to foster in their children an awareness of their
choice-making abilities. When they demand freedom from
rules, parents must remind them that they are and always
have been free to do exactly as they choose. But they
must deal with the consequences of their choices. Those
consequences are set by parents and by society. By learning to function successfully within a framework of family
discipline, rules and limits, children acquire the self-
control and decision-making ability essential for healthy
adaptation to the adult world.

In addition, healthy parenting has to do with what is on
the inside of kids, not the material things provided for
them, nor even the outcomes of their choices. Parenting
should encourage a process of living that reflects an emphasis on the internal values that govern behavior and
guide choices. An old Chinese proverb states, "Give a man
a fish and feed him for a day, teach him how to fish and
feed him for a lifetime." Parents frequently instill dependence, low self-esteem and irresponsiblity in their children
by giving them answers without encouraging them to use
their own abilities first, by providing material luxuries without encouraging work, by granting privileges without expecting responsibility, and by setting limits without giving
consequences for violations of these limits.

We know what you're thinking. You have read all of
this background material outlining societal changes, the
concept of adolescence as a stage of development and
myths. But you still don't know what to do when your
children make bad grades, get depressed, yell and act ob-
noxious. Don't worry. We're getting to that now. The
foundation for a healthy, effective approach to parenting

today's adolescents is found in the principles and philosophies outlined in the next chapter.

These principles are designed to give parents a proactive, not reactive, approach to guiding their adolescent's transition from childhood to adulthood. Our principles are consistent and clear, and can be applied to a number of situations ranging from typical adolescent problems to the more severe types of problems encountered by an increasing number of parents. Also, these principles can be applied not only to today's society, but to parenting issues for years to come.

5

The 10 Commandments Of Healthy, Effective Parenting

Now that you've read the background material which is critical to *understanding* the process of parenting adolescents, it's time to move on to the guidelines. Notice that the 10 Commandments talk about healthy effective *parenting*, not controlling adolescent behavior or producing perfect children.

We strongly encourage you to consider these guidelines in developing your own philosophy of parenting, recognizing that your goal is to provide a family environment that communicates the love and caring you feel toward your children in a manner that encourages them to grow toward responsible maturity and positive self-esteem.

Effective parenting refers to what you can do as a parent to provide this environment. The emphasis is not on controlling your children's behavior as much as it is on providing a *loving, healthy reality*.

Let's face it, parenting is hard work. Most parents love their kids and want them to be happy and it is often difficult to do what is best for children when that is different from what they want.

Consider the following example and examine your initial reaction:

Jennifer's mother found cigarettes in her daughter's pocket while sorting the laundry. In response to her mother's confrontation, Jennifer became angry because she felt her privacy had been invaded. She then screamed that the cigarettes did not belong to her, but to a friend. What should Jennifer's mother do?

CHOICES

1. Believe the explanation about the cigarettes belonging to a friend and apologize for the invasion of privacy.
2. Realize that Jennifer is merely going through a normal rebellious phase, ignore it and be thankful that she is not pregnant or using drugs.
3. Deliver a three-hour lecture on the hazards of smoking, complete with slides of damaged lungs.
4. Tell Jennifer how hurt, disappointed and rejected she (mother) feels, and ask where she failed as a parent.
5. Ground her from all privileges for six months.
6. None of the above.

This typical scenario illustrates the uncertainty parents feel as they attempt to deal with their adolescent's struggle toward maturity. All of the choices above, although exaggerated, are commonly selected by parents and advocated to some degree by various self-help books and mental health professionals. However, we think the correct answer is 6, none of the above. To understand why, parents need to incorporate the following principles into their parenting approach. After reading the Commandments, re-examine your thoughts about the options presented here. The above scenario is discussed at length at the beginning of Chapter 6.

COMMANDMENT 1

Trust Your Instincts, But Know Yourself

When people have children, they automatically become responsible for the development and welfare of others instead of just themselves. And while most adults have this intellectual awareness, they fail to understand that a prerequisite for raising stable, strong and well-adjusted individuals is to possess those same qualities themselves.

Most healthy parents have survived and even mastered many difficult situations. As a result, they have developed a firm system of values, an adequate level of self-esteem and the ability to make good decisions. Their behavior meets our definition of maturity. That is, they generally do what is best, even if it's different from what they want. Thus, parents' own maturity and judgment will be their first guide to deciding what is best for their children.

However, even if parents are mature, they still are human. As such, they probably have made some decisions which, in hindsight, reveal their imperfections. Perhaps they are divorced, single parents, have to work long hours, had children at an early age, are recovering alcoholics, were abused as children, etc. The point is, just because they are not saints and may not be storybook parents, they need not discount their own maturity, experience and the right to make decisions about their children.

At the same time, achieving maturity involves experiences that will have influenced parents' personalities. Parents have needs, feelings, issues, conflicts and problems. That's okay. What is not okay is to be unaware of these personal issues and how they affect an individual's role as a parent.

For example, parents who undergo difficult, conflict-ridden divorces and are now single or remarried may feel they have deprived or injured their children. While this may be true to a certain extent, it is a mistake to overreact and become overly permissive in an attempt to compensate. This may soothe parental guilt, but does not benefit the child. Similarly, working parents may feel compelled to spend all of their free hours pleasing their children in an attempt to pacify their belief that their children are starving for parental attention. Some parents have such excessive needs for approval that they do not set effective limits for fear their children might reject them or be angry.

Parents who had difficult childhoods and had to work hard for everything they got may constantly push their children. More often, however, these parents vow that their children will never have to suffer what they did, so they indulge their kids in an attempt to spare them a painful childhood.

Parents who are the products of rigid, strict, work-oriented upbringings tend to expect orderly, predictable and overly compliant behavior from their own children. When their kids respond with impulsive, imperfect — in other words, typical — behavior, these parents attempt to mold their children and force them into roles that are unrealistic for their age or unique personalities. This combination is frequently seen in abusive parent/child interactions.

Yet another example of parents with strong issues of their own are parents who had their children when they themselves were still teenagers. Teenage parents who still need parenting themselves have much difficulty meeting both their own childish needs and the needs of their children. By the time their children have reached adolescence, relationships between parents and children are more like siblings than parent and child. Setting limits becomes extremely difficult because these parents are not viewed as authority figures.

Then there are biological parents who have not had custody during the childhood years, who then become primary custodial parents when children hit adolescence and begin acting out. These parents, usually fathers, try to make up for years of absence by being totally giving, understanding and loving. Adolescents usually exploit and manipulate this situation.

These are a few typical scenarios; many other variations are possible. But problems are not created by the fact that parents are imperfect. Problems occur when parents lack knowledge, awareness and understanding of their own feelings, values and issues. When this happens, a parent's conflicted judgment tends to hamper and impede the healthy parenting process. Parental issues need to be balanced by self-awareness.

The ability to separate personal issues from the process of deciding what is best for a child is often referred to as "detachment." When parents lack this detachment, several warning signs may indicate that parents are beginning to "lose it." These warning signs include extreme feelings of anger and frustration much of the time. A similar warning sign is feeling powerless in interactions with adolescents. Excessive feelings of guilt or pity for a child usually precede poor parental judgment, as does over-identification (parents seeing too much of themselves) in their kids. However, the most common emotional precursor to poor parenting is uncertainty.

Unfortunately many parents are unsure of themselves and their ability to do the right thing. Of course parents hear and worry about drugs, teenage suicide, teenage pregnancy and peer pressure, but they get unbelievably diverse messages about how to help their adolescents deal with these pressures.

When parents are unsure, they often, like adolescents, respond to peer pressure. For example, a mother decided to say no to her 12-year-old son watching an R-rated movie from the video store. When the child complained that all the other kids' parents were letting them watch it, she decided to prove to her child that this was not so. To her surprise and dismay, she discovered after calling the other parents that her son was right. Other parents were allowing their children to watch the movie — even though the children were five years under age.

The Two-Mistake Test

This is a permissive society. Many times parents will do what is easiest, not what is best for their kids. Parents cannot necessarily trust what other parents, and especially kids, say is right. Parents need to go with their own instincts. If unsure, they can always take the most conservative path.

The *two-mistake test* is a helpful tool. In the case of R-rated movies, look at the consequences of saying no to such movies, when yes would be okay. In this example, this 12-year-old would have the consequence of not enjoying a movie and perhaps not being able to identify with those friends in this situation. The other choice would be saying yes to the movie, when no would be better. A yes would expose this 12-year-old to a level of sex, profanity and violence (that is why a movie is rated R) that could result in or compound a variety of problems including sexual anxiety, guilt and inadequacy, or even thinking that sex among teenagers is desirable and okay. In addition, since the code specifically states that R-rated movies are not for individuals 17 and under, this decision gives children the message that it is okay to break the rule. Also, by saying yes in the face of parental peer pressure, parents teach that it is okay to give in to peer pressure. If parents are truly dedicated to the task of raising honest, responsible individuals, which mistake would they rather risk making?

COMMANDMENT 2

Don't Sacrifice Your Own Happiness For Your Child

Children learn about the adult world and what it means to be an adult by watching the adults they know (Mom and Dad) live their lives. Their knowledge of what it means to be a mother, father, husband, wife, man or woman comes primarily from watching their parents in each of these roles. In this respect, all parents are teaching a class on adulthood. When it comes to this class, children are quite attentive.

Parents teach their children not so much how *to* live but how *they* live. Often how parents live is heavily influenced by what they learned from their own parents. Parents can only teach what they know. Parents also remember issues, problems or desires from their own upbringing that motivate them to be different in some ways from their parents and to raise their own children somewhat differently.

It is important to look at the subtle messages about adulthood that are given to children by the lives their parents lead. One concept passed on from generation to generation is the idea that children should have it better than their parents did when they were children. Whenever parents say this, they frequently are referring to the materialistic aspects of family life. Parents may defend the need for both to work out of economic necessity, but also to provide those highly sought-after luxuries because their children want these things. When asked, kids do indeed want an unlimited allowance, a car at age 16, unlimited free time and trendier clothes. Don't forget, immaturity is marked by pursuing wants to the exclusion of choosing what is best. That is normal in childhood. It is no surprise that children support their parents' desire to have it better than when they were kids.

However, what is best in fostering the development of healthy values and self-esteem should not be decided by immature children, but by parents whose judgment should be better. Parents frequently complain that they work hard, deny themselves luxuries, and spend all of their free time chauffeuring kids, cleaning up after them, and solving their problems, only to be greeted with a lack of gratitude and a strong sense of entitlement from those children. These same parents are shocked when their children state they don't want to be adults or mothers or fathers or wives or husbands, because those roles don't look very rewarding.

When parents work hard to make their children happy, they unconsciously expect their children to work just as hard at making their parents happy. Thus, parents expect reciprocity. Reciprocity implies that doing something for others elicits kindness in return. While most parents understand intellectually that reciprocity is not to be expected in parenting, they tend to expect it emotionally. Thus, many parents feel that they give and give to their children and get nothing back. Frequently, increased efforts at even more giving follow, with parents mistakenly believing that they must be doing something wrong if their children are not responding to these offerings.

Unfortunately increased giving is often met with an increased sense of entitlement from adolescents. An adolescent desperate for a car and given a nice, used car by his parents might complain about the inadequacy of the stereo. Adolescents may feel it is a parental obligation to provide cars and the least they can do is give them a decent stereo.

Many parents attempt to build their whole lives around the goal of making their children happy. They tend to tie their self-esteem and feelings of adequacy to their role as parents and evaluate their success as parents on the basis of how happy their children appear to be. However, happiness to immature children is typically defined as satisfying wants. Children do not easily relate to the adult concept of happiness, which includes healthy values, good relationships, work and responsibility.

In many families, parental self-worth is so tied into their children's happiness that parents lose sight of themselves as individuals and tend to live their lives vicariously through their children. These are the same parents who suffer the painful "empty nest" syndrome when their children leave home. They then realize they have not cultivated their adult relationships. Parents cannot expect to motivate their children to become responsible adults if their children's view of adulthood, parenthood or marriage is bleak and unrewarding.

One of the best gifts parents can give to their children is their own positive self-esteem. If adults don't acknowledge or take care of their own needs and pursue a fulfillment that is meaningful and rewarding to them, they find they have taught their children by example that misery, discontent and self-sacrifice are all that is to be expected from adulthood. Parents are individuals and they are husband and wife, as well as heads of the household. Each of these aspects of their lives needs attention if healthy, successful family adjustment is to be attained.

COMMANDMENT 3

Know Your Child. Listen To The Words, Trust The Behavior

To be effective parents, it is as important to know your children as it is to know yourself.

"But Doc, I see my kids every night at supper. Sometimes we watch TV together. Last summer we even took them on vacation with us. Of course I know my kids."

Unfortunately parents assume that their superficial observations of their children's behavior is actually a true indication of who and what their children are like. Understandably, it is much easier for parents to assume that all is well rather than look below the surface and possibly find things that might be cause for concern. But the need to really know a child is more critical during adolescence than at any other time.

Adolescents can become extremely involved with their own needs, feelings, desires and peer group. As they begin to form their own personalities, develop their own values and make decisions, they naturally find part of this process to be in conflict with parental wishes. As a result they may withdraw, become secretive or present an image to their parents based on what the parents want to see.

Children are not always what they appear to be. When parents are not around, kids can be totally different. Around their parents or other adults, adolescents may be polite and obedient, leading adults to the conclusion that all is well. Naive parents often discover too late that their

children have been engaging in destructive or inappropriate behavior. Effective intervention at that time is often
difficult and outside help is frequently needed to remedy
the situation. When parents mistakenly believe and accept
a false presentation, they give up the opportunity to intervene and influence that adolescent's growth process in
constructive ways. This allows adolescents to raise themselves, which often leads to destructive ends.

This brings us to the issue of trust. *We believe no adolescent
can be trusted 100 percent.* Why? Not because adolescents
are naturally devious, deceptive or dishonest, but because
adolescents are *immature.* Adolescents constantly have to
choose between what feels good to them and what is
acceptable to parents. Immaturity means that in some
situations, wants win out. This is normal.

It is not unlike the situation in which a parent tells a
four-year-old not to play in the street. That four-year-old
may say that she will abide by this rule, but when the ball
rolls out into the street, what happens?

While parents readily assume that four-year-olds cannot
be trusted and supervise them accordingly, parents often
lose this understanding when dealing with teenagers.
They forget that trustworthiness is predicated upon responsibility. An adolescent's level of trustworthiness
needs to be based upon their level of responsibility, maturity and honesty. This level will vary dramatically with
different children. Also an adolescent may be much more
trustworthy in situations such as school, than with
members of the opposite sex.

Adolescents quickly learn that most parents have an
innate need to trust their children and to think the best of
them. Perhaps this is because most parents mistakenly
associate trust with love and caring. They believe that if
they love and care about their children, they also need to
trust them. An overly trusting attitude on the part of
parents teaches adolescents engaged in destructive behavior that saying what parents want to hear is an acceptable
substitute for responsible behavior. Adolescents can be-

come very good at talking appropriately while acting inappropriately.

However, if parents make assumptions and evaluations about adolescents based not on words, but upon behavior and performance, adolescents become responsible for being positive people, not just good talkers. For parents to do this, they must have working knowledge of what their adolescents actually do, not what they say they do.

This information can be obtained in a number of ways. One way is to spend sufficient time with an adolescent to make an accurate assessment. Arrange to be around adolescents in a variety of situations. Parents should observe their adolescents in school activities, with peers and around other adults. Parents should assume that adolescents don't always act the same way around their parents as they do around others. To find out how their adolescents act around others, parents should talk to other people: other parents, teachers, group leaders and even their adolescent's friends.

This brings up a controversial point. Are parents willing to invade their children's privacy and get information without their children's knowledge? We believe the answer to this question needs to be *yes*. If adolescent behavior is causing parents to be uncomfortable or to question an adolescent's trustworthiness, parents need to waive their children's right to privacy.

Adolescent privacy is a privilege dependent upon demonstration of positive behavior.

If parents seriously question their child's honesty, they not only have a right, but an ethical obligation to investigate. This investigation may include room searches, locker searches, purse searches, reading notes, listening to phone conversations or even urine drug screens. Parents must answer the question, "Which is more important, my children's privacy or their lives?"

We realize that adolescents need privacy. Time alone and unsupervised interactions with friends are important.

But evidence of destructive relationships, inappropriate sexuality, affiliation with negative peer groups, or alcohol or other drug use must be investigated. An adolescent involved in negative behavior will deliberately mislead, deny and hide this information.

Similarly, another important way of trusting behavior is to monitor and check-up on where adolescents are and what they are doing. Parents cannot trust that just because another parent is present, their children are being adequately supervised. Parents need to routinely talk with parents of their adolescent's friends, making sure that the values and expectations of other parents are consistent with their own.

Parents should love their kids unconditionally. They should love them when they are good, bad, imperfect, nice, honest and dishonest. But trust should not be unconditional. Trust must be based upon responsibility, consistent honesty and trustworthy behavior. As such, trust is relative and a matter of degree. Love should be unconditional. Trust should not.

COMMANDMENT 4

Build Positive Values At An Early Age

Changes in American society have led to a dramatic lack of consistency and structure in its institutions and their ability to teach healthy values effectively. We are referring to the traditional values upon which this country was founded — honesty, responsibility, success through hard work, self-discipline, caring and treating others as we would like to be treated. Without consistent, structured presentation by families, schools and churches, adolescents tend to look to the media and peer groups for information about what is right and important in life.

Children tend to lack true values in the sense of a stable internal guide for behavior. Behavioral control is primarily external. For an infant, all control is external. Parents feed, bathe, nurture and define limits to all activities. As thinking and physical ability develop, it is the interaction of children with parents that first defines the limits of appropriate behavior. The values that guide behavior for children are therefore external and defined by parents. Feedback from parents in the form of external consequences, both positive and negative, is a child's first exposure to a value system.

The more stable the presentation of a value system by parents, the stronger the development of an internal value system can be in adolescents. A stable presentation provides a foundation for the internalization of values that must occur for responsible maturity later. Adolescents with stable and strong value systems will better cope with and survive typical pressures. It is important for parents to provide experiences that facilitate development of such values.

This goal requires parents to set positive examples so kids can do as they do, not do as they say to do. Children model behavior they see in their parents. A live demonstration of an activity is always more dramatic than a report or verbal guidance. Which is more effective: telling a child how to tie a shoe or showing him? Other life lessons are taught in a similar manner. If parents make excuses and bend the truth, kids will too. If parents abuse drugs and alcohol, abuse each other and act irresponsibly, kids will do the same. "Listen to the words, but trust the behavior" applies to parents as well as their children.

Another principle in the process of building values is setting clear and consistent expectations for children, because what is expected by parents usually turns into what is believed by adolescents at a later age. If parents tolerate dishonesty, irresponsibility and immediate self-gratification, children will expect and be satisfied with the same type of behavior. Many times, parents will tell their teenagers they should be honest and responsible, but parental behavior indicates that parents will accept the opposite. This is the case with parents who consistently bail their kids out of trouble, make excuses for them and are satisfied with minimal work and effort. These parents unknowingly succeed in raising *KWASOMs* (Kids Without Any Self-Discipline Or Motivation). KWASOMs are given everything but accomplish little on their own. KWASOMs have low self-esteem and fail to mature because they do not possess values or the ability to delay immediate gratification.

Parents need to help children learn that life is sometimes frustrating, that good things do come to those who wait and that true satisfaction comes from effort, giving and caring about others. In particular, parents need to teach children that every positive behavior does not have, nor does it have to have, an immediate payoff. While we believe in teaching kids how to manage and be responsible for money, constant bribes and rewards for appropriate behavior result in adolescents forming an unrealistic belief that all efforts will be consistently and immediately rewarded — a principle totally unrealistic in the real world of employment and adult relationships.

Finally adolescent values are heavily influenced by the groups of which they are members. At the same time, adolescents have a limited number of options when choosing groups within the youth culture. Therefore, it is vital for parents to encourage and even direct adolescents toward positive group activities. A positive group activity is one that incorporates compatible values and emphasizes effort, responsibility and cooperation. These activities are not always easy to find and often require initiative from both parents and adolescents. Positive groups are available through schools, neighborhood organizations, sports programs and churches. Involvement in organizations with positive values may be the best insurance, although not a guarantee, that parents can buy to protect against adolescent involvement in destructive behavior.

COMMANDMENT 5

Emphasize Willingness, Effort And Emotional Risking

All children are not born equal. Children arrive in this world each with their own unique set of talents and abilities. Since kids are not born with equal talents and abilities, focusing on external achievement is the quickest route to problems with self-esteem. A focus on external achievement reflects an emphasis on outcome or result. Result-oriented approval does not take into account that children do not share equal talents or that they each may not be capable of the same range of results. Straight As seems to be a widely shared parental goal, yet not all kids are capable of it.

Society is externally oriented, technologically oriented. Why? Because it is psychologically and emotionally less complicated to focus on the outside of a human being than the inside. More and more in today's society, an individual's success is measured not by maturity level but by a tally of acquisitions. Even in relationships, emotional intimacy is frequently traded for matching Rolexes. Families focus on the right clothes, house, car and gadgets to the exclusion of family time and activities. In this externally oriented society, things have replaced people. Self-worth has become an issue not of who people are and what they believe in, but rather what they have and what they own.

There is a solution. The answer lies in rejecting external validation of a person's worth and embracing an internal value system. The universally shared ability to give 100 percent lies in the internal arena. Regardless of talent or intellect, all people have the ability to give 100 percent in their efforts. This factor forms the building blocks of self-esteem. Any time people are willing to give 100 percent, they will feel good or better about themselves. Unfortunately, society in general and parents in particular don't always reward or praise effort; they only praise outcome. To build self-esteem based on internal values, this must change. Although outcomes are not always completely under an individual's control, effort is.

Lack of effort frequently reveals a lack of commitment. Language used to relate to the world can often stimulate or weaken commitment to the task at hand. The old saying "can't never could" applies here. Words not only describe situations or feelings, but reinforce them. A good example is the phrase "I'll try" in response to a request.

In today's society, "I'll try" is used as a sign of commitment. But to "try" is appropriate only when individuals are unsure of their ability to attempt or accomplish a task. In our work with adolescents, we have defined "trying" as "the time spent deciding whether you will or whether you won't." When was the last time, Mom or Dad, you were invited someplace you didn't want to go. Rather than be honest, you stated "I'll try to make it," knowing full well that keeping that particular commitment (and thus not lying) required no effort beyond uttering those words. Children know all too well that "I'll try" has become an excuse. However, parents accepting this response to a request or directive are amazed when the garbage is not taken out, the room not cleaned or when the grades don't improve. Parents can reinforce commitment by saying to children, "Are you willing to do it or are you just going to try?"

"He's a bright child but he's making lousy grades" is a frequent complaint. In this situation, forget grades for the time being. What does his effort look like? What is his daily approach to school? Rather than focusing on academic outcomes and responding to report cards, parents need to focus on children's effort and willingness. Children can be successful each and every day they keep to their study plan. Given adequate intellectual ability, the right effort will produce appropriate grades. We say appropriate because they may not be the grades parents want, but if children give their best effort that, coupled with their academic ability, will produce what they are capable of producing.

Parents should ask no more than what children are capable of giving. We think more of and have more respect for kids who give 100 percent and make Cs than those who give 50 percent and make Bs. This is what is meant by praise for internal, not external, self-worth. Focusing on the value of hard work gives each child an opportunity to succeed, because any child is capable of hard work. Too many times children's spirits are dashed when they give 100 percent but do not get the external result they seek. One hundred percent effort should be considered success in its own right and praised as such by parents. If the goal is accomplished, that can be considered an extra.

To build healthy self-esteem, adolescents must also take emotional risks. Emotional risking refers to an adolescent's willingness to deal with uncomfortable situations. Adolescent development is filled with anxiety, emotional pain and uncertainty. This is a normal part of any growth stage. Emotional risk-taking is therefore critical to the transition from childhood to adulthood. Mastering an uncomfortable situation may not be possible for all adolescents but the willingness to risk facing an uncomfortable situation is certainly an option open to all. Facing discomfort, fear or uncertainty is another way for a teenager to feel successful regardless of outcome. The willingness to risk is self-affirming.

How many parents have not heard at least one of the following reasons (excuses) for not doing what is healthy, positive or growth-producing? "It's too hard," "I'm scared," "I'd be embarrassed," "The kids will think I am a nerd," "It will take too much time." The typical parental response is a lengthy statement on how the situation isn't really that hard (embarrassing, scary or time-consuming). This robs adolescents of an opportunity to learn what they are capable of handling. The subtle plea by teenagers is that they shouldn't have to do something if it is too hard, too scary, too embarrassing, etc. Trying to talk teenagers out of their feelings encourages the idea that something being difficult, scary or embarrassing is a justifiable excuse for not exerting the effort.

A much more effective parental response is, "Are you willing to do it, even though you are scared, even though it is hard or even though you would be embarrassed?" This not only encourages responsible behavior but lets adolescents know that their parents view them as capable. In addition, the above response accepts their feelings, which is self-validating, and gives parents an opportunity to praise any indication of appropriate effort.

The following poem reflects these issues in a most eloquent way:

To laugh is to risk appearing the fool,
To weep is to risk appearing sentimental,
To reach out for another is to risk involvement,
To expose feelings is to risk exposing the self,
To place ideas and dreams before the crowd is to risk loss,
To love is to risk rejection,
To live is to risk dying,
To hope is to risk despair,
To try at all is to risk failure,
But risk we must,
Because the greatest hazard of all is to risk nothing,
For those who risk nothing, do nothing, have nothing, are nothing.

Anonymous

COMMANDMENT 6

Be A Parent Not A Friend

Somewhere in the midst of the social liberalization that began in the '60s, society seized upon the idea that it was more important to be a friend to a child than to be an authority figure. This idea was probably perpetuated by authors of permissive child-rearing books who scared parents into thinking that behaving like authority figures would produce a crop of hopeless neurotics or another Hitler. As a result, many parents are quite firm in their defense of the friendship theory and their favorite rationalization is, "If I'm not his friend, he won't come to me when he needs to talk to someone." Another popular defense is, "If I'm her friend, she will talk to me more and then I will know what she is really doing." Our personal favorite is, "If I am an authority figure and say no, they will get mad and rebel even more."

Parents who want to be friends to their adolescents usually are needy themselves. They may be in distant, unrewarding relationships with adult partners and attempt to compensate for what is missing in their adult relationships. Similarly, parents who live for their children often befriend their kids rather than form other adult relationships or develop appropriate outside interests. Single parents are particularly vulnerable if they do not have any other rewarding relationships outside the family. Other "friendship" parents befriend their adolescent in an unconscious desire to be young again, thus avoiding their own midlife issues. Parents also typically befriend adolescent children in a last-ditch, unconscious effort to have more closeness at a time when children are in a normal stage of pulling away.

Whatever the reason, for the friendship theory, experience shows this belief can be an invitation to child-rearing disaster. Parents can be friendly with their kids, but never friends. Those who see themselves as friends to their 13-year-olds need to ask how many other 13-year-olds outside their family they consider friends and part of their social circle. Parents need friends and adolescents need friends, but neither parents nor adolescents should need each other as friends.

Adolescents are typically insecure and uncertain due to the extreme changes they are undergoing in their lives. As such, they have an underlying emotional need to view those who care about them as stronger and more powerful. Viewing parents as more powerful and in control provides adolescents with an anchor for their changing feelings and beliefs. If parents abdicate this role in exchange for friendship, adolescents feel more lost and out of control. These inner feelings may not be visible because, on the surface, they seem to get more freedom and privileges from friend/parents. But while seemingly happy with this situation, adolescents typically will be searching for the missing powerful parents, perhaps replacing them with a negative peer group or a rock star. Parents have a responsibility to meet their children's need for a higher power, and the primary way parents serve this function is by setting limits.

Friendship requires liking and limits usually are not that likable. Webster defines a friend as "a person on the same side in a struggle." Authority, on the other hand, is defined as "the power or right to give commands." People who set limits often are not liked. Therefore, parents who set limits must be willing to give up popularity and friendship in exchange for authority. The situation is similar to the relationship between boss and employee. Bosses must be willing to sacrifice being liked to make decisions that are best for their organizations.

Parents are capable of having extremely close, intimate relationships with their children, and we have personally facilitated interactions between parents and adolescents characterized by amazing amounts of honesty and caring. However, even in these situations, parents are loving and friendly authority figures for their adolescents, not friends. Parents can and need to be supportive, as are friends. Parents need to be sensitive, as are friends. Parents may sacrifice and do what is best for another person, as do friends. Sound parenting involves many of the same characteristics as good friendships. But companionship and liking should not be the goal of the parent/child relationship during the adolescent period. Adolescents need structure, and friendship must often be sacrificed if appropriate limit setting is to take place.

Also in the '60s, society began a "rights" movement that continues today. During that time, society became aware that almost every conceivable subgroup of the American population was victimized in some way by other groups in society. Thus, ethnic groups, women, the mentally ill, the handicapped, homosexuals and various others justifiably charged inequality and discrimination. Discrimination against children also became a central issue and very positive legislation originated from this movement; legislation such as child abuse laws and a child's right to appropriate special education services. However, during this process, many children and their parents also came to believe that children have equal rights with adults. This belief led to major problems in the areas of discipline and childrearing practices today.

When parents assume equality between themselves and their children, they are demonstrating belief in the miniature adult theory. Parents subscribing to this theory unconsciously assume their children have the same levels of morality and judgment as mature adults. Parents, therefore, are inclined to extend the same privileges and opportunities to their children as to themselves. Similarly, parents typically apply the same rules and expectations to themselves as to their adolescent children, thus having "equal rights."

When kids discover that their parents are concerned with being equal, it creates a golden opportunity for manipulation. Adolescents are now able to push for adult privileges, while having only a child's level of responsibility.

For example, adolescents confronted for smoking or drinking under age are quick to reply, "Well, it's okay for you to smoke and drink, why can't I?" Adolescents who join negative peer groups tell their complaining parents, "You have no right to set limits on my friends, I don't pick yours." If parents accept the assumption that rules and privileges should apply equally, they will naturally fall prey to this type of argument. As a result, equal parents grant privileges and opportunities totally inappropriate to the maturity level of their kids. At other times, these parents make such ridiculous compromises as, "I'll cut back on my drinking if you cut back on yours."

When confronted with equality arguments, parents should remind kids of the high level of parental responsibility and maturity that allows them as parents to make choices if they are willing to take responsibility for the consequences. Thus, parents also have the right to make unhealthy choices, smoking for example, and adolescents can be reminded that when they reach the appropriate level of legal and emotional maturity, they too can make unhealthy choices without suffering parental consequences.

We believe children are entitled to the same amount of *respect* as adults. But this is where equality ends. By virtue of their age, status, maturity and level of responsibility in life, parents have a level of freedom that is far greater than children. This responsibility and moral obligation to do what is best for children gives parents the right to set limits, impose consequences and assert authority. This is an exclusive parental right. When parents recognize that adolescents are not miniature adults and are not equal, they are in a position to help their kids learn that "rights" come from responsibility, maturity and self-discipline. Parental love is helping children to understand that privileges are a direct result of responsibility. The truly caring parent will value the importance of this lesson much more than playing the tit for tat game with an adolescent about equality.

The net result of equal parenting is much the same as friendly parenting. Adolescents are given a level of freedom and opportunity inconsistent with their level of judgment. This combination often is a recipe for unachieved potential, low self-esteem and a destructive lifestyle.

COMMANDMENT 7

Set Limits. No Is A Complete Sentence

While children are becoming physically mature at increasingly early ages, intellectual, social and emotional maturity is still incomplete. Even more importantly, adolescents lack a stable system of internal rules (values) to guide them consistently on their journey to adulthood. Both experience and common sense indicate that adolescents are not miniature adults, nor do they possess an innate guide to appropriate development. Therefore, it is critical that parents master the practice of setting limits to prepare their children to function in the real world.

Limits are representations of the real world and as such are an important opportunity for adolescents to deal effectively with their environment. Through limits, teenagers learn to deal with frustration, disappointment, boredom, rejection and anger. Limits also help adolescents appreciate that emotional pain and discomfort are not necessarily determined by events, but by the way individuals respond to those events. For example, adolescents learn that it is their choice to react to a no by arguing, pouting, complaining or by accepting the situation and making the best of it. Through limit-setting, adolescents give up the mistaken notion that freedom means no restrictions. Instead they realize that a more appropriate definition of freedom is the awareness of one's ability to choose. Parental willingness to set firm limits enables adolescents to become more aware of choices and their consequences. If maturity is defined as "the willingness to choose what is best when what is best is different from what one wants," parental limits serve as a constant index of what is best, even though it may be different from what adolescents want.

Another reason for setting limits, beyond fostering maturation, is to maintain order in the family. As stipulated in the second commandment, parents have a right to their own happiness. This won't be realized if they are constantly cleaning imaginary tire marks off their backs because their kids are running over them. As an ancient Chinese philosopher once said, "Parents who are afraid to put their foot down have children who walk all over them."

Understanding the need to set limits is important; learning to do it is another thing entirely. For example, parents who tell their 15-year-old that he can't go somewhere on a weekend night, are likely to be asked immediately, "Why not?" Parents may mistakenly believe that the "Why not" is a request for information and an explanation of how they arrived at the decision to say no. Parents may reward this request for further information by launching into a lengthy discussion. However, teenagers are rarely interested in explanations; they are interested in getting their parents to change their minds. (If adolescents were truly interested in explanations, they would ask for them after receiving a yes as well.)

How many parents have heard, "Why do I have to come in so early when all my friends get to stay out later?" However, we have yet to hear of an adolescent who has asked his parents, "Why do you give me this privilege when none of my other friends get to do this?" In general, "Why not?" is an attempt to manipulate, not a reflection of adolescent yearning for knowledge and understanding.

Adolescents typically engage in any number of attempts to change the parental system, most of which result in some kind of argument. Why do parents argue with their kids? For some strange reason, many parents believe (mistakenly) that they must not only defend and justify their position on a matter, but that their adolescents have to agree with it. Attempting to justify, defend or explain sends the message that parents might not be sure of their position, that the issue is up for negotiation. If parents are unsure of their position, it's okay to say so, invite the adolescent's opinion, and then make a decision. Once parents begin arguing, teenagers get a foot in the door and it becomes a no-lose situation for them. If adolescents are allowed to argue, they have the opportunity for three destructive payoffs. First, parents may become frustrated, give up or even get out-debated, thus allowing their little lawyers to have their way when their own way is not best. Second, even if the answer remains no, adolescents have succeeded in getting a considerable amount of attention for negative behavior, thus increasing the probability that it will occur more often in the future. Finally, even if the answer remains no, adolescents succeed in causing much frustration and anger in their parents. This results in an unhealthy feeling of power for adolescents, which is also a payoff.

We therefore emphatically urge parents to realize that no is a complete sentence. It requires no defending, no explaining, no justifying. We encourage parents to give themselves permission to say no and to feel good about it for no other reason than that they would be uncomfortable saying yes. Saying no in this manner helps teach adolescents that sometimes there will be limits with which they will have to deal, regardless of whether they feel those limits are fair.

In addition, when parents say no because they are uncomfortable saying yes, they are modeling the importance of sensitivity to feelings. If every no has to be backed up and justified, the implication is that feelings don't count and do not form an adequate basis for saying no. Is there a parallel for an adolescent attempting to refuse a beer or marijuana with "No, I don't feel like it" and being met with "Why not?" by his peers? If he has been taught by his parents that all no's require rational explanation, he may feel at a loss to back up his no and thus be more responsive to peer pressure.

COMMANDMENT 8

Discipline, Don't Punish

A close partner to the process of setting limits is the broader concept of discipline. For many parents, discipline equals punishment. Punishment is a very personalized, often aggressive act toward a child that functions more as a means of channeling parental frustration than as an attempt to teach or influence adolescent behavior.

We prefer to think of discipline in less negative but more constructive terms. We define discipline as feedback from the environment that informs adolescents that their approach to living, as represented by their choices, is not healthy and/or effective. The purpose of discipline is to promote learning, not to cause children pain.

Let's look at how inappropriate and ineffective many traditional parental control techniques are. One old parental standby is yelling and screaming. Parents reason that because they hate to be screamed at, adolescents will feel the same and cease the negative behavior. In reality, adolescent behavior is rarely affected by this process. In fact, adolescents usually feel powerful and in control when parents yell and scream. Kids sometimes test limits just for the fun of seeing their parents out of control.

Often yelling and screaming turns into threatening. But when parents make threats while they are angry, adolescents are liable to dismiss them for what they are — emotional and illogical attempts at control. Adolescents know unrealistic threats will be withdrawn when everything cools down. Much of the time, parents feel so stupid and guilty after such episodes that they will reward children in some half-hearted apologetic effort. If anything, adolescents see yelling bouts as opportunities to increase their control over their parents.

Another traditional means of attempting to control adolescents is the lecture. Parents who lecture, preach and moralize are unconsciously adhering to the miniature adult theory, operating under the mistaken notion that adolescents share the same level of morality and motivation as lecturing parents. But adolescents are characterized by thinking disorders and immature value systems. Therefore, the normal adolescent response to a lecture is to *act* interested, ashamed and guilty. When the lecture is over, parents feel better, but teenagers learn nothing about consequences.

A related and equally inappropriate means of attempting to influence adolescent behavior is guilt-tripping. For example, parents say they will be very hurt and disappointed if their adolescents engage in a particular behavior. However, since many adolescents have poorly developed senses of morality to begin with, a guilt-trip does not lead them to refrain from a particular behavior. Instead, they may begin to resent their parents for trying to manipulate their emotions.

When all else fails, some parents resort to physical (corporal) punishment in a last-ditch effort to stop problem behavior. This approach is often the beginning of a potentially dangerous cycle of family violence. This approach works worse with adolescents than with younger children. To begin with, even if physical punishment does stop the problem behavior, that behavior will cease only if the kids believe they will be caught, and the effect of such punishment is temporary. In addition, adolescents feel extremely humiliated and resentful when they are physically disciplined. These feelings are likely to be channelled into violence either toward parents or outside the home. It is difficult to imagine a situation in which corporal punishment is an effective and lasting solution to any problem. If an adolescent's behavior is so out of control that physical restraint needs to be used, this is an indication that discipline in the traditional sense will not be effective, and some type of outside intervention is necessary.

Behavioral Contracts

Rather than using such ineffective means as yelling, lecturing, guilt-tripping or physical force, we recommend a form of discipline that draws upon the principles of cause and effect and developmental psychology. This approach is best represented by use of a written behavioral contract. The concept of contracts guiding and governing behavior certainly is not original. In fact, society functions constantly under a variety of contracts, most of which are implicit. Human behavior in the context of marriage, job, school and place of residence is all of a contractual nature.

A contract is an agreement between two parties. The agreement concerns the rules or limits used to govern the relationship between these parties. Since our society is built upon the concept of contracts, it seems logical to have contracts to describe and specify the rules and limits that apply to behavior in relationships between parents and adolescents.

Using a specific written contract has several distinct advantages. First, it serves as a clear statement regarding parental beliefs, values and expectations. It helps to reduce arguments, misunderstandings and manipulation. In addition, a contract keeps parents from having to constantly make decisions about rules on the spur of the moment or in the face of pressure from their teenagers. By writing out a contract, adolescents can clearly see that their behavior and choices have definite and predictable consequences. Thus, parents are viewed as less punitive since they are simply carrying out their part of an agreement, not punishing the child in a subjective, personalized manner.

When adolescents sign a contract, they are agreeing in advance to accept a set of rules. This process increases the amount of personal investment and commitment from adolescents, reducing the adversarial aspect of relationships between parents and themselves. Also, adolescents feel a greater sense of power and control over their destiny when they know and understand the terms of their contract.

The first section of a contract should be addressed to rules, expectations and responsibilities of adolescents. They need to be concise, and specific. Often, there is an advantage to dividing rules into categories, i.e., attitude, school, relationship with friends, household responsibilities, clothing, music, sex and drugs. Differentiating major from minor offenses is often helpful. Associated with every rule should be a statement regarding consequences for violating that rule. Generally, consequences should be restrictive in nature. If possible, the restriction should be related to the irresponsible action. If a curfew is violated, adolescents should be given an earlier curfew or prevented from going out for several days. Restricting phone, TV, stereo, car use, socialization and allowance all can be effective. In general, more intense, brief consequences result in more learning than do indefinite consequences, which are apt to lose their potency and be repealed prematurely. The goal is to negatively impact adolescents, not parents. Consequences must therefore be realistic and enforceable.

A particularly effective type of consequence is the time out (TO) or learning experience (LE). This well-established technique requires the adolescent to spend approximately 15 minutes in a quiet environment for self-reflection. An adolescent's room (without TV, stereo or phone) will serve the purpose. A learning experience (LE) is a helpful intervention in response to such attitude problems as arguing, yelling, disrespect, begging or whining. This self-reflection period can further facilitate learning if the LE is "processed" in writing (see Appendix G).

After the consequences section of a contract, many parents find it helpful to include explanations or philosophy statements. This section can describe the purpose of a contract, and it tends to put contracts into perspective for adolescents.

Finally, contracts should contain a section for signatures of all parties. An adolescent's signature indicates understanding of the terms of the contract, not necessarily agreement. A sample contract is included in Appendix B.

After a contract takes effect, parents and teenagers should set a regular time to discuss it and make any necessary modifications. During these discussions, parents can take the opportunity to compliment their children in any areas of progress and maturity, ultimately leading to increased responsibility and privileges. At the same time, parents can point out areas of irresponsibility, adding more restrictions as needed. With this process, parents can continue to show adolescents that freedom is the awareness of one's choices, rather than life with no restrictions. However, contracts should be altered only at meeting times, not in the heat of an argument or confrontation. Whenever a contract is unclear or ambiguous, parents decide the intent of the contract and the terms that apply.

Actually, written contracts can be used with children as young as four or five. Of course, in early childhood years, this process is more simplistic and relative to a child's level of maturity. In some cases, written contracts are not necessary if all parties clearly understand and agree to those rules and conditions in existence. However, our experience indicates that unwritten contracts should be the exception rather than the rule.

Please keep in mind that contracts cannot control adolescent behavior. Only adolescents can do that. However, contracts and the principles they contain do guide the process of discipline and limit-setting by parents, thus helping struggling teenagers toward their ultimate goal of maturity. Contracts also make the maturation process more observable, allowing parents to judge and evaluate more accurately the extent of maturity in any particular area. Likewise, contracts increase adolescent self-esteem as they reflect upon their success and achievement relating to compliance with contract terms. Finally contracts reduce the amount of family focus on limits and discipline, allowing more time for supporting, sharing, communicating and enjoying.

COMMANDMENT 9

Talk, Don't Communicate

Whose problem is this? In the last 20 years, psychologists, educators and self-help book authors have been quite frank about telling parents that they, not their kids, have communication problems. Parents are led to believe that they possess some kind of learning disability that hampers their ability both to talk and listen to their children effectively. Many times these resources encourage adults to get down on the child's level. Parents become convinced that if only they can learn to communicate with their kids, everything will be okay.

In fact, communication theories seem to embrace indirectly the "friendship" and "parents and kids are equal" theories, as well as the "miniature adult" notion. Also the communication approach places all responsibility — and blame — on parents. Effective parenting is much more complex than simply learning to communicate, as we have been demonstrating in this book.

Although many parents have difficulty communicating love and firmness, we believe the importance of verbal communication theories has been overemphasized. There are, however, some basic rules about communication that, when combined with the other principles outlined in this book, can make guiding adolescents to maturity a little easier.

Communication with adolescents can be broken down into two major categories. The first category involves asserting authority and setting limits, while the second category includes the ability to engage in general discussions and normal conversation. Both types are very important and represent ways in which parents show love, caring and guidance. The second category however, could be termed as more supportive, while the first is more closely associated with the authority role.

The Authority Figure

To communicate effectively as an authority figure, parents need to keep in mind the other Commandments, especially the previously explained principles of Commandment 6 (Be a parent not a friend, kids and parents are not equal) and 7 (Set limits: no is a complete sentence) when speaking with adolescents.

Consistent with these principles, effective parents need to communicate with adolescents in a manner that demonstrates authority and leadership. A calm authoritative tone of voice is essential. A tone of voice hinting of uncertainty indicates to adolescents that a particular issue is up for negotiation.

In addition to an appropriate tone of voice, effective parents also need to concentrate on using words that indicate authority rather than friendship. Words like "expect" and "will" are preferable to such words as "please," "wish," "want," "prefer" or "hope." Clearly adolescents receive a very different message from the statement, "I expect you home at 9:00," than from the statement, "I wish that you would try to be here by 9:00."

On some occasions, after setting a limit or expectation, parents may choose to remind adolescents of particular consequences if they do not comply with the limit. (Reminding adolescents of specific consequences should not be confused with making threats.)

Another important point in setting limits is for parents to choose appropriate times to make authoritative statements. For the most part, rules and consequences need to be outlined in advance, as in the case of contracts. When this is not possible, parents should speak with adolescents at a time when teenagers are reasonably calm and unemotional. Parents need not discuss limits and consequences when adolescents are extremely angry, upset or obviously looking for a fight. Similarly, parents need to avoid making disciplinary decisions when they are feeling emotional and irrational themselves.

Much of the time, adolescents push for explanations. In some situations, when an explanation will help teenagers to accept a particular limit, parents may choose to briefly explain the rationale behind a decision. However, explanations should be brief and take into account an adolescent's developmental level. For example, it is unrealistic to expect a 13-year-old to understand why she cannot date until she is 15. On the other hand, some 16-year-olds may be able to understand why parents do not want them to smoke cigarettes.

If adolescents indicate that they are either unwilling or unable to understand an explanation, parents can stop the explanation process immediately. Adhere to the 30-second rule. This rule stipulates that parents need spend no longer than 30 seconds attempting to explain a rule, limit or consequence. Any explanation longer than 30 seconds will almost always be repetitive and result in lecturing or moralizing. Also after 30 seconds, adolescents typically begin arguing or quit listening.

Another common yet self-defeating communication technique which typically occurs shortly before the discipline and consequences, has parents asking *why*. For example, an adolescent who is discovered to have lied about his whereabouts is asked, "Why did you lie to me?" When parents ask why, they are looking for a mature explanation as to why a particular immature behavior occurred. In essence, they are asking for a mature explanation of immature behavior. When adolescents reply with an equally immature answer such as "I don't know," parents feel even more frustrated.

In these situations, parents actually encourage adolescents to fabricate an answer or give the "I don't know" response. If parents really thought about why their adolescent did a particular thing, they would realize that they, the parents, are in a much better position than adolescents to answer the question. Most of the time, the true answer is either, "Because I wanted to," "Because it felt good," or "Because it helped me avoid pain or discomfort." So the real question is, "Why do parents ask why?"

Supportive Interactions

In raising adolescents, a considerable amount of time needs to be devoted to interactions that do not involve asserting authority. Many parents get so bogged down with control issues that they fail to take time to engage in normal, healthy interactions with their children. While these normal interactions can be extremely rewarding for both adolescents and parents, they are still very different from adult to adult conversations. Thus, to communicate effectively with adolescents, parents need to keep several principles in mind.

To begin with, parents need to be available for normal conversations. In too many families, the only time parents and teenagers interact is when adolescents want something or when parents need to assert authority. Parents need to spend enough unstructured time with their adolescents so conversation can occur naturally. Unfortunately, many times when adolescents begin to open up and talk, parents feel compelled to direct, control, interrupt or pass judgment. If every time adolescents begin to talk they are met with advice or a value judgment, then of course they will respond by not talking around parents. It is important that parents concentrate on listening and reflecting, rather than directing and giving advice.

For example, when adolescents begin talking about feelings of isolation and rejection because they don't fit in a particular peer group, this is not the time for parents to launch into, "It doesn't matter what everyone else thinks." Another common mistake is for parents to interrupt with advice on the mature and logical way to think and feel. In the above example, a more appropriate response would be, "You sound pretty frustrated right now." This simple reply acknowledges and accepts an adolescent's feelings and encourages more disclosure than a lecture or pep talk.

In many situations, adolescents just need an understanding ear and empathy, not problem-solving. To a teenage girl who says, "I'm just not as pretty as the other girls in class," many parents would respond with a superficial, "But we think you are beautiful" type of remark. They might buy her new clothes or send her to modeling school. But statements like, "How you look is really important to you right now" are much more effective than advice because they acknowledge her feelings of insecurity without contributing to them.

An adolescent boy who studied six hours for an algebra test only to make a D says, "School is too hard." Too many parents would rather debate with him about how hard school is instead of validating his feelings with the response, "It hurts more when you really put forth effort and still don't meet your expectations."

Once parents realize that lecturing is not appropriate, they may then attempt to relate on an adolescent level by sharing stories and personal experiences. This technique can be helpful occasionally, but for the most part it is viewed by adolescents as a lack of understanding. Parents can be more effective by learning to communicate with their adolescents on a feeling level.

If teenagers have parents who communicate feelings effectively, then not only do they have permission to communicate their own feelings, but they have increased respect for their parents' willingness to be human.

This is further enhanced if adolescents see their parents communicating with each other on a feeling basis without losing control. Parents who say, "I am really feeling frustrated with my job right now" are much more effective than those who take it out on the kids or hide in their room for an hour after getting home. (Expressing feelings in front of adolescents should not, however, be confused with using adolescents as sounding boards for personal problems, a process that is clearly destructive and inappropriate to a healthy parent-adolescent relationship.)

A final common communication problem is the tendency for parents to be too serious. When parents take themselves and their children too seriously, the joy and spontaneity of everyday life is diminished. Adolescents become so involved with their own feelings and problems that they lose perspective and have a hard time seeing the lighter side of life. Parents need to make an effort to show their children the lighter side of everyday living.

COMMANDMENT 10

Take A Stand On Sex And Drugs

Too many experts making contradictory statements about childrearing has led to a "human chameleon" phenomenon in parental value statements. A chameleon is a lizard which can change its skin color to blend in with its environment. It does this to protect itself from predators. Many parents feel they live in a predatory society and feel a need to protect themselves from scorn. They often change their views and their lifestyles to fit in with what is current and fashionable. They become human chameleons, blending in with the social environment and refusing to take a stand on anything of significance.

Self-esteem comes from knowing what values (colors) are important. Parents cannot foster healthy identity development in their children if they are constantly changing their own values to fit in. Children suffer less and benefit more from parents who take unpopular stands than from parents whose values are always open to debate and the whims of a confused society. Parental stands provide an anchor for children. Whether adolescents admit it or not, knowing exactly where their parents stand on issues is comforting and provides a strong sense of security. This is true even if kids are in firm opposition to the stand taken. Loving, powerful parents seen as authority figures are absolutely vital in the tumultuous world of adolescents frightened by their developing sexuality, independence and choices. Again, it is critical to remember that children know where their parents stand on issues by watching them live their lives. A publicly presented value unmatched by parental behavior will destroy parental credibility.

Adolescents experiment with sex and drug use at a much earlier age in today's society. Many parents give up, saying no one can stop adolescents from doing what they are going to do anyway. And while it is true that taking a stand will not guarantee an end to behavior contrary to parental values, parents must be willing to take stands on issues that affect their children.

Sexual activity and drug use are volatile subjects. Parents feel a lot of anxiety in dealing with these subjects openly. Statistics show that virtually all adolescents experiment with sex and drugs, so many parents accept it as part of normal development. Statistically, a majority of kids also lie, steal and cheat at one time or another during their adolescence, but these behaviors are not accepted with resignation because society has more clearly defined values relating to dishonesty, theft and cheating. Parents typically have better defined limits related to these behaviors than they do to drug use and sexuality.

Parents must reflect their values about sexual activity and drug use to their children in the form of clearly defined limits of allowable behavior. Parental limits provide standards about which adolescents will make choices and experience consequences. This is the anchor to which adolescents relate. No drug use of any kind, including alcohol use, is appropriate for adolescents. Clearly defined consequences for use of alcohol and other drugs should be delineated and strictly enforced. Also, keep in mind that alcohol use is still *illegal* under age 21. Information designed to aid parents in detecting such problems is included in Appendix C.

In the same vein, as immature beings, young adolescents are not ready for or capable of engaging in responsible sexual relationships. While society is preoccupied with superficial sexuality, parents must emphasize that any sexual expression by adolescents has tremendous impact on their feelings about themselves and weighs heavily in their adjustment. Sexuality is an extremely important component of a developing adolescent's identity. Premature sexual relationships can be very damaging to their fragile self-esteem. This is doubly dangerous in that many adolescents engage in premature sexual relationships out of a desire for emotional intimacy and to shore up low self-esteem — only to end up with just the opposite result.

Since much of the stimulation that pressures adolescents into early experimentation with sex and drugs comes from TV, movies and the music industry, it is imperative that parental values be clearly defined in these areas even if in direct contrast to what is considered acceptable by society. Much of the media stimulation aimed at adolescents is increasingly bizarre and deviant. Distorted images of sexuality, aggression and the unusual are used to attract adolescent attention. Therefore, parents must provide healthy standards to balance this unhealthy pressure.

A difficult distinction is differentiating between what is distasteful to parents — "I can't believe they like that noise" — and what truly is a rejection of healthy parental values. While acknowledgment of parental distaste might lead to stretching the bounds of parental tolerance, media stimulation that rejects parental values and promotes drug use, promiscuity and violence should be dealt with through parental limit-setting.

Take a stand based on your values. Your children are *your* responsibility. Use this book to help you with your thinking and ideas, but above all, take a stand that is your own and reflects your values. In this commitment you model an approach to life that is valuable to your children.

In the Commandments we have attempted to break down the relatively complex, highly individualized process of parenting into basic principles and guidelines. In doing so, we are offering an approach that applies to numerous situations, a large variety of problems and a very wide age range. In fact, many parents report that these principles apply quite well to preadolescent children. At the same time, adolescence presents some unique challenges to parents, and traditional parenting approaches developed around the early childhood years are, in our minds, just not sufficient.

Because of an adolescent's strong need for structure, our principles tend to emphasize heavily the limit-setting aspect of the parenting process. Limit setting is a critical component of a parent's love at this age. However, we do not intend to minimize a parent's need to demonstrate love through involvement, physical affection and sharing. It all goes together.

6

Applying The Principles

 In this chapter you will learn how to apply the principles of successful parenting through a series of questions and answers based on real-life scenarios.

Question 1

When I was sorting laundry, I found a partially used pack of cigarettes in pants belonging to my 13-year-old daughter Lisa. I asked her about the cigarettes and she became angry with me for invading her privacy. She then said they belonged to a friend. Everyone tells me that all teenagers go through this phase and I should just let it pass. What should I do?

Answer

Your response to this typical adolescent situation will indicate to Lisa how you will respond to future violations of parental and societal limits. First, under no circumstances believe the ridiculous explanation that they belong to a friend. This is the oldest excuse in the book. You would be extremely naive to believe it and would be viewed by Lisa as gullible.

Regarding her charge that you have invaded her privacy, remember that you discovered the cigarettes by accident, not by snooping. However, despite the circumstances of this discovery, remember that privacy for an adolescent is a *privilege* based upon demonstrated trustworthiness and honesty, not an automatic *right*. By becoming involved in an argument with Lisa on the issue of invading her privacy, you will be caught in a "bait and switch" situation, dealing with your behavior rather than hers. In any confrontation, you need to stay focused on her issues, not yours.

Also keep in mind Commandment 3, "Know your child. Listen to the words, trust the behavior," when any situation arises where the explanation offered by your adolescent is inconsistent with the evidence of dishonesty. You should proceed as if your daughter is experimenting with smoking and decide on appropriate action.

Concerning your friends' statements that all teenagers go through this phase, we would again point out that all teenagers also go through phases of lying, throwing tantrums and arguing with their parents. However, parents certainly wouldn't let those incidents pass, nor can you ignore this situation just because you wish that it would go away. In fact, whether it passes or not depends largely upon how you react to this first incident. Your reaction will indicate to Lisa how you will respond to the use of other drugs or participation in illegal activities in the future. Don't fall for the "it's-just-a-stage" fallacy.

When you confront Lisa, she may argue that she should be allowed to smoke since you do. Remember that parents and kids are not equal. (Commandment 6, "Be a parent not a friend.") She will naturally test limits and experiment with behaviors different from parental values. Remember also that she has a need to look older and fit in with her peers.

Keep in mind that Lisa is not a miniature adult. Her understanding of the dangers of cigarette smoking is not on the same level as yours so refrain from delivering a lecture on the hazards of smoking. Also refrain from attempting to produce excessive feelings of guilt or shame by talking about how hurt and disappointed you are. Finally, do not overreact or punish her for an unrealistic period of time.

Instead refer to the written behavioral contract in which you clearly expressed your values and the behavior you consider acceptable in the area of smoking. If you have not yet developed a written contract, let her know very clearly that you disapprove and will not accept this type of behavior. Inform her of the consequences for a first offense of this type, which probably needs to be some type of grounding and withdrawal of privileges. Discipline, don't punish.

You might also make an attempt to find out which of her friends smoke so that you can more closely monitor her peer group. Consider restricting her from peers who smoke. You can also inform her that since her trustworthiness has decreased as a result of this incident, you may be checking her room and purse on occasion to make certain that this does not occur again. If she yells or throws a tantrum during this interaction, provide appropriate consequences for this particular type of behavior as it occurs, keeping it separate from the original incident. Refrain from constantly bringing up the incident and moralizing about it after initial confrontation.

Question 2

My 14-year-old son, Ron, is starting to hang around with a couple of boys who look sloppy and rough. We also have noticed that he is very secretive about these friends and meets them away from home. When we try to talk to him about this, he cuts us off saying we have no right to pick his friends.

Answer

Initially it's important to express your concern directly. Let your son know that you view this as a problem requiring change on his part. He can deal with your concern by bringing his friends home and introducing them, or arranging for you to meet with their parents. Make it plain that the only other option for dealing with your concern is limiting his social interaction outside of school to activities that are parent-supervised.

The interest you show in meeting his friends and talking with their parents is effective in telling your son that you love him enough to be interested in his activities, whether he is directly supervised or not.

If Ron refuses to accept these limits or agrees verbally but does not follow through, then consider a professional evaluation. A family system is functional when appropriate rules are generally followed or consequences are accepted when rules are broken, and learning from such mistakes is evident.

Determining whether what you see is destructive is important. Your feelings of discomfort are enough to warrant further evaluation on your part. Friends whose appearance is objectionable to you may or may not reflect a problem requiring intervention. For further help in evaluating your son's friends, see Appendix E.

Adolescents experience a variety of influences, both positive and negative. How Ron handles these influences will reflect whether he needs intervention. If his behavior is positive most of the time, then chances are he is handling the influences in his life fairly well. However, if he is exhibiting a significantly more negative attitude, a deterioration in values, or a decreased level of responsibility at home or in school, then your son may not be handling outside influences appropriately, and parental intervention is necessary.

Question 3

I am worried about my daughter Sherry, 15, who comes home from school almost every day depressed because she says her clothes are not as good as all the other kids at school. She seems very concerned that her hair and makeup are different and that "the other kids in my class all have VCRs" and she is the only one who doesn't. We are working parents who cannot afford to buy her everything she wants, but I don't want her to be unhappy. How should we approach this?

Answer

Because she is an adolescent, Sherry is feeling very insecure and self-conscious, and her primary solution to this feeling is trying to gain acceptance from her peers. At the same time, peer acceptance from adolescents generally is based upon such external things as clothes, cars and appearance rather than personality characteristics such as achievement, caring or the ability to be a good friend. Sherry believes that if she can dress and look like her friends, she will be accepted and will feel less anxious.

Part of Sherry's depression is caused by her adolescent thinking disorder. It is obvious to most adults that clothing, hairstyle and VCRs are not the true road to happiness. Also, Sherry thinks irrationally when she expresses the mistaken belief that "all" the other kids at school have "stuff" that is better than hers. Whereas her perception is that everyone else it better off, she is probably somewhere in the middle; some kids have more, some kids have less. Don't be surprised if fact-based explanations fail to change her perceptions.

In responding to this situation, it is important to implement those techniques discussed in Commandment 9, "Talk, don't communicate." Your daughter seems to be looking for reassurance and understanding. This can be accomplished with statements such as "I know it is important for you to be accepted by your friends right now, and it must really hurt to feel that other kids are better than you." At this point, you might also share some of your own feelings as an adult surrounding these same issues, i.e., an inclination to keep up with the Joneses. However, avoid at all costs lectures that could turn into some version of "I had to wear rags to school when I was your age." Also refrain from comments that make Sherry feel stupid for having the feelings she has.

While responding with understanding, however, it also is important that, in acknowledging her strong need to be accepted, you do not sacrifice your own financial situation (Commandment 2: Don't sacrifice your own happiness for your child). If you give in to her wishes in this area, you are reinforcing her childish belief that self-esteem comes from external, material things, rather than from within. You also reinforce her mistaken belief that as parents, you are primarily responsible for her happiness rather than for teaching her appropriate coping skills. In doing so you are subscribing to the myth that, "Problems and unhappiness are bad for children." Allowing Sherry to experience feelings of rejection and not fitting in or not having as much as someone else gives her the opportunity to deal with such feelings, since these are issues she will be facing for the rest of her life. You might use her strong need for better clothes to suggest she get a job babysitting to buy more of the clothes she wants. That would channel this typical adolescent concern into participation in a work ethic and help her to "build positive values at an early age" (Commandment 4).

When responding to Sherry's depressed feelings, try to assess the degree to which these feelings are a typical response to situational stress or if these feelings reflect a more serious problem with depression. Focus on the frequency of such statements and how long the moods last. Do her moods respond to reassurance? Other signs of depression include sleeping difficulties, poor appetite, excessive withdrawal, crying spells and statements indicating hopelessness and despair (see Appendix F). If these signs are present, seek professional evaluation.

Question 4

I have read that kids now start using alcohol at a very early age, and I don't want to be irresponsible in this area. I have been thinking of allowing my 17-year-old son Martin to drink beer with me at home on the weekends and let him observe me drinking responsibly to teach him to do the same. Is there anything wrong with this?

Answer

Yes! While it's tempting to use an adult yardstick when seeking solutions to problems of major concern with adolescents, drug use *of any kind* is extremely destructive. Alcohol remains the most destructive drug of choice for adolescents, and it's important that parents do not give mixed messages about whether it is appropriate for adolescents, which it is not. Kids also start experimenting with sex at an early age, but parents wouldn't apply this same approach to sexuality.

Alcohol is illegal for those underage. This is a rule with which teenagers obviously disagree, but it remains a reality that they must learn to deal with. (Review Commandments 7, "Set limits. No is a complete sentence," and 10, "Take a stand on sex and drugs.")

Teenagers frequently say, "If you want me to act like an adult, then you should treat me like an adult." This seems to make good sense to many parents. However, what an adolescent is asking for is not adult responsibilities, but adult privileges. Parents and children are not equal in responsibility and need not be equal in privilege. Responsible drinking by still-developing adolescents is impossible.

While you cannot control Martin's choices, as a parent it is important to model your values, your respect for the law and how you handle limits on your behavior. For your son, any alcohol consumption is illegal. This reality needs to be reflected in your behavior. It is important that you model the belief that alcohol consumption by anyone under the legal age is not allowable and meet any violations of this rule with appropriate consequences. Also, rest assured that your son's alcohol use with his friends is much different than it would be under your supervision. Underage drinking is, by definition, illegal and irresponsible; therefore, responsible drinking by an adolescent (your son) is impossible.

Question 5

My daughter Michelle, who is 15, refuses to do anything that my husband, (her stepfather), asks her to do.

We have been married three years. The first year we did not push the issue, but now my husband feels he should have some authority over her and respect from her. When we try to talk to Michelle about this, she says, "I don't have to do anything he says because he's not my real dad." How should we handle this situation?

Answer

This is a very common situation in today's blended families. How the role of stepparent is handled is critical not only to an adolescent's future development, but to the functioning of an entire family. Realistically Michelle cannot be expected to view her stepfather as a replacement for her natural father, and it also is not realistic to expect her to like or love him to the same degree. However, stepparents *are* entitled to the same respect as adults and as authority figures.

Many times divorce creates feelings of guilt and hesitation on the part of natural parents, and they are defensive and slow to expect adolescents to respect and accept stepparents as authority figures. This situation is fertile ground for manipulation by adolescents, who quickly realize that the stepparent situation presents opportunities for resisting parental authority. It can be even worse if the noncustodial parent, in this case the natural father, does not support stepparent's authority.

Because each blended family is very different, it is difficult to formulate a consistent plan to deal with every situation. In the example described, we would emphasize that, yes, your husband does have every right to be respected and accepted as an important person and an authority figure in the home. However, if your husband expects Michelle to love and care about him to the same degree that she does her natural father, he will most likely be very disappointed. Therefore, let Michelle know that both you and your present husband will be asserting authority and making rules, and you expect her to follow them. Remember Commandment 6, "Be a parent not a friend."

As the custodial natural parent, make certain you do not become a middle man (or woman), constantly intervening in battles between your husband and your daughter, or taking sides. If possible, call upon your ex-husband to support the authority role of your present husband, letting your ex-husband know that this is in no way an attempt to take anything away from his relationship with your daughter. Otherwise insist that your daughter follow the rules stated in her contract, and provide consequences as a team. Contracts are an especially effective tool in blended famlies. First, because they reduce the potential for inconsistencies between how natural parents and stepparents handle individual situations. Secondly, they help divorced parents agree in advance to procedures for intervention in potential problem situations.

In responding to Michelle's excuse of "He's not my real dad," you need to indicate your awareness of Michelle's attempt to manipulate by saying, "The issue here is not who is a real dad. The issue is compliance with authority. In this house, your stepfather and I make the rules and expect them to be followed. In your dad's house, he does the same. In the classroom, your teacher is in charge." A final statement could be, "If you have some issues or problems about your stepfather's role in this family, we would be happy to discuss them at another time."

If Michelle argues further or continues to show disrespect, apply time-outs or other behavioral consequences such as loss of phone use, grounding, etc. as specified in the contract.

Question 6

My son Barry, age 12, just brought home Cs and Ds on his report card. He made low grades on his second report card, and I took away his phone privileges until the grades improved. He assured us that he was making good grades this six weeks, but this report card was even worse than the last. He just doesn't seem to be interested in school and all he thinks about is his friends. What should I do?

Answer

First of all, it is important to understand that Barry's greater interest in his friends is completely normal. Immaturity is characterized by doing what one wants at the expense of what is best. It is easy to see that Barry is pursuing his wants (friends) rather than what is best (school). At 12 Barry remains quite immature. Your concern is a reflection of your mature understanding of the importance of academic success for Barry's future. Barry is more interested in his friends today than in some vague concept of future success. Your approach to this problem will model the distinction between what is best and what is wanted.

It is important to understand that you cannot make Barry do well in school. You can only provide the opportunity and present the expectation. (Review Commandment 5, "Emphasize willingness, effort and emotional risking.") You provide the opportunity by structuring Barry's time. We encourage parents to focus on their children's approach to school and their daily effort, as opposed to long-term outcomes, which is what a grade at the end of a six-week period represents. Since Barry has indicated by his behavior that play is more important to him than school, his priorities must be addressed. This can be done by establishing a study period that occurs prior to play, right after school, before he goes out to visit with friends, or after dinner, before any TV, stereo or phone calls are allowed. It is important to realize that you can only structure the time — you cannot make him absorb information. He must understand through your actions that you consider school important, and that you will structure his time and priorities if he is unwilling or unable to do so. Thus you have made a value statement to your child about the importance of school.

After you have established an academic plan with Barry that provides structured opportunity for study, it is important to assess if he is using this time productively. Make yourself available to Barry at the end of each study period to process some of what he has done to see if he is using the time to study and work or is daydreaming. Do this for the first week or two of the new program. Also, call his teachers to find out if they see a difference.

It is important to rule out learning disabilities or other problems that may be interfering with his ability to function at school. If consultation with school and attempts at home-study restructuring make no improvement, further evaluation is indicated.

Question 7

Terrye, my 14-year-old daughter, has withdrawn from the family. Until last year she always came home from school, had a snack and told me about her day at school. Now she rushes past me in a blur, goes straight to her room, closes the door, turns on the radio and gets on the phone. She seems only to come out for meals or to go out, and she totally ignores her five-year-old stepbrother, whom she used to adore. I am worried about her. What should I do?

Answer

It sounds as if Terrye is probably experiencing a relatively normal adolescent process of being very preoccupied with herself and her friends. During the period of early adolescence, kids begin forming an identity separate from parents by secluding themselves to some degree and reducing their exposure to parental influences, while increasing their involvement with peers and peer-related activities such as music.

It also sounds as if you, like many parents, have been very involved with your daughter during her childhood, and you are therefore prone to personalize her behavior and feel rejected by her as she goes through this relatively normal process. Your feelings in this area may be a signal that you should take a look at how much of your own self-esteem is based upon a close relationship with your daughter. Be careful not to interpret Terrye's normal need for privacy and her own world as a personal rejection of you. As you struggle with this issue, you may also find it helpful to become more involved with other people and outside interests, since Terrye's tendency to separate will continue as time goes on. The first Commandment, "Trust your instincts, but know yourself," is certainly applicable to this situation.

While examining your own feelings and increasing your understanding of the normal adolescent process, you might also attempt to regulate the degree of Terrye's withdrawal to some extent. For example, you might mandate that her phone be taken out of her room until she shows somewhat more balance in her level of involvement with the family. Consider limiting the amount of time she can spend talking on the phone and listening to the radio, and you might further insist that she spend some time each day involved in activities with the family, even if it is just watching television. All of these suggestions can be incorporated into a behavioral contract. Resistance on Terrye's part needs to be met with both firmness and understanding of her increased desire for independence, using techniques discussed in Commandment 9, "Talk, don't communicate."

Concerning Terrye's disregard of her younger stepbrother, this too is very common for girls beginning adolescence. Whereas before reaching adolescence, girls often model their mothers and therefore seem to enjoy a parental role with younger siblings, girls often give up this role as they become preoccupied with themselves and insensitive to the needs and feelings of others. Although this is normal, think about increasing Terrye's interaction with her stepbrother by rewarding appropriate involvement such as babysitting with increased freedom outside the home.

You need to anticipate less involvement on her part with the family at this point, and you may have to begin making changes in your own social activities as a result. If her withdrawal reaches a point at which you suspect she could be seriously depressed, refer to Appendix F for additional signs. Similarly, if you suspect she is involved with destructive friends or activities, remember to "Know

Your Child. Listen to the words trust the behavior" (Commandment 3) as well as referring to Appendix C on adolescent drug use and Commandent 10, "Take a stand on sex and drugs."

Question 8

My 16-year-old son, Ken, has a habit of coming home about 15 minutes past his curfew. When his curfew was 11:00 p.m. he said it was too early and not comparable to his friends, and that was why he was late. As a compromise, we extended his curfew to midnight. This worked fine for a while, but then he started coming in late again. How should his stepfather and I handle this problem?

Answer

Violating curfew is a common limit-testing technique. When confronted, kids want to focus on the fact that they were "only a few minutes late," instead of the fact that they were late at all.

More often, kids will have a variety of reasons why they were late and why no consequences should be applied. But children who are held accountable for their behavior are more likely to become responsible adults, while those able to rely upon a variety of excuses tend to become "good talkers." Commandments 3, "Know your child. Listen to the words, trust the behavior," and 4, "Build positive values at an early age," are certainly important here. In the real world, excuses (even legitimate ones), don't count for much. Actions and behavior are remembered long after excuses are forgotten.

Clearly there will be times when unforeseen, legitimate circumstances necessitate a late arrival. But these are few and far between and fairly easy to distinguish if it's the rare occurrence.

The important issue is not how many minutes late, but the unwillingness to take responsibility for being home on time. Focus on responsibility. One minute or one hour late is still a violation of the curfew and a reflection of irresponsibility. It is just as easy for Ken to be home ten minutes early as it is to come home late. It is a matter of choice, priorities and motivation. Letting curfew violations slide without consequences gives Ken the message that it is okay to be irresponsible as long as it is not by much.

Curfews set by parents are limits, about which their children will make choices. Your adolescent's handling of limits within the family is a good reflection of how he will handle limits later in life. Parents cannot control their children's choices, but they can provide reality reminders in the form of consequences. An adolescent who violates curfew should experience an earlier curfew on the next social outing. Repeated offenses suggest that time away from home needs to be restricted due to obvious irresponsibility.

Question 9

I think my 16-year-old daughter Jenny is having trouble with her relationships with boys and sex. She has had a series of older boyfriends, hangs around with an older crowd and dresses provocatively. I have found more than one note written to a girlfriend with strong sexual references. Once I overheard her talk to a friend about a pregnancy scare. What should I do?

Answer

From the information you have gathered so far, you have every reason to be seriously concerned about your daughter's involving herself in potentially destructive relationships and situations. Given these concerns, it is important to recognize that privacy is a luxury that you cannot afford to give Jenny at this point, when her health and well-being may be threatened by her activities. Privacy is a privilege that is earned through responsible decision making. You need to find out exactly what is going on.

Since destructive relationships and irresponsible sexual behavior are frequently associated with alcohol and drug abuse, you need to look for signs that your daughter is involved in other forms of destructive behavior as well. If her level of honesty is a concern, it is important to "Know

Your Child. Listen to the words, trust the behavior" (Commandment 3). Clearly state or restate family values regarding sexual behavior and other behaviors of concern including drug use, curfew violation or participating in unsupervised activities.

Let Jenny know that because you love her and have concerns about her apparent poor judgment in these areas, you will be limiting her opportunities for unsupervised activities, implementing limits on out-of-school and weekend activities, and monitoring her compliance as a means of assessing her ability to make responsible decisions.

If what you have observed is just the tip of the iceberg, Jenny will probably not comply with the new limits and that may well precipitate a crisis. If she is unable or unwilling to comply, then you need to consider some form of professional evaluation.

Question 10

My 15-year-old daughter Jane recently came home with alcohol on her breath. When we confronted her she lied, but later admitted that she'd had "one or two" beers at a party. How should we handle this?

Answer

Drug use is one of the most dangerous activities with which adolescents experiment. It's critical to respond firmly and in a manner that clearly states that no use is acceptable. (Refer to Commandments 7, "Set limits. No is a complete sentence," and 10, "Take a stand on sex and drugs.") Many parents think experimentation with alcohol is a typical part of growing up and feel comfortable with a stern lecture to their children when the situation arises. However, most adolescents tend to view the lecture or the emotional outbursts less as consequences for their choices and more as a form of "overhead." Adolescents frequently view lectures as a sign of their parents' disagreement with their actions as opposed to a statement that such behavior is wrong. Parents must respond to wrong behavior with reality-based consequences that are also behavioral. If the alcohol use (wrong behavior) occurred within a context of no adult supervision and with friends, then the consequence needs to be one of being grounded for at least one week under adult supervision. Follow this with an additional period of only those activities that can be easily monitored by parents. This is an indication to Jane that since her choices with her friends without adult supervision were irresponsible and destructive, her behavior will be restricted to insure her safety.

It is easy to focus on the alcohol use and overlook the fact that Jane lied to you. The dishonesty should also be addressed and reponded to with a consequence. This way you are making the value statement to your children that drinking is wrong and that dishonesty is also wrong.

While responding firmly to Jane's alcohol use, this would also be a good time to sit down and explore some of the pressures and dynamics of the situation that resulted in her choice to use alcohol. (This, of course, needs to occur later and not while Jane is experiencing any alcohol effects.) Perhaps Jane needs help in dealing with pressure for peer acceptance and developing alternate strategies for remaining drug-free. If she is uninterested or unwilling to discuss this with you, then it is important to make the no-use rule clear as well as the consequences for violating the rule.

Question 11

Our 15-year-old son, Wayne, has difficulty accepting our rules and authority. Every time we try to discipline him or ground him from friends or activities, he gets irrational and threatens to run away. At other times, he says, "You never let me do anything. Life is just not worth living. I'd rather be dead than live in this house." We are scared to death and concerned that we are being too strict with him. What should we do next?

Answer

Situations like this are certainly very difficult for parents because overreaction on the part of adolescents leads parents to question their judgment. Wayne's threatening, blaming reaction in response to your limits is probably manipulation designed to do just that . . . make you question your judgment. It is more likely Wayne is having difficulty with judgment and impulse control, not you.

When adolescents threaten in the context of limit-setting, they are almost always attempting to produce parental fear and doubt, hoping that parents will relent and compromise a rule, a limit or a consequence. So it is unlikely that your limits are too strict, and it is quite apparent that Wayne has some rather significant problems. However, it is possible for parents to be overly strict or harsh in their parenting techniques. Therefore, parents can check their attitudes and behavior against the warning list included in Appendix D.

It is apparent that Wayne is suffering from a number of adolescent thinking errors such as a tendency to jump to conclusions, all-or-none thinking and emotional reasoning. But whenever adolescents are in such an emotional state as to make self-destructive threats, parents need to consider getting some type of professional evaluation and intervention.

However, Wayne's apparent overreacting could mean that limits and consequences have not been clearly articulated as in a written behavioral contract. If not, a contract might not only reduce the degree of his resistance, but it will also guide you in your attempts to apply appropriate consequences for violation of limits that have already been discussed and accepted.

In general a family situation is working when either rules are being followed or consequences are being accepted when rules are not followed. Learning is taking place. However, whenever teenagers are unwilling to deal effectively with either the rules or the consequences, the situation approaches an out-of-control point. When this happens, parents also need to look at other areas of an adolescent's functioning — school, friends, and alcohol and drug use — all of which could be major factors in the problem.

An initial intervention in the situation above might go something like this. After Wayne has spent some time in his room cooling off, you might say, "Wayne, we are extremely worried and concerned about your inability to handle yourself when you make these kinds of threats and become so out-of-control. If you continue to feel this desperate in response to our limits, we are willing to find you some outside help so you can learn to better handle your feelings. If there are other things going on in your life that you think we need to know about, we are happy to listen. However, our limits are firm and are not up for negotiation."

Question 12

I am concerned about the music my 13-year-old son Paul listens to. I was shocked when I finally managed to understand the filthy words in one of the songs. I can't believe the way these rock stars look on the posters in his room. Lately he has taken to wearing concert T-shirts with awful-looking creatures on them who look violent and aggressive. Can I do anything about this?

Answer

We encourage parents to take a stand on what is allowed in their homes based on their values. (Re-read Commandment 10, "Take a stand on sex and drugs.") Rock music groups have one goal and that is to sell records to your teenager. To do this, they become increasingly bizarre, violent, sexual and deviant to attract your child's attention. We encourage you to investigate the music Paul is listening to. Read the lyrics, and closely examine any posters of rock groups that may be hanging in his room. What is merely distasteful and reflects age-appropriate differences can be ignored. Anything reflecting negative, destructive attitudes that violate family values needs to be removed by parents. Family values need to be clearly stated to children. You may not be able to control what your child listens to outside your home, but you certainly have an opportunity to define family values by placing limitations on music and possessions within your home that reflect negative values.

A preoccupation with negative heavy-metal music filled with themes of death, destruction, sexual deviancy and Satanic overtones often signals a troubled child needing professional intervention. Any time you see behavior and attitudes that reflect intense attachment to and glorification of a particular rock group or type of music, find out what that group is like and what their music is about. Rock stars are frequently heroes to today's youth and can be quite influential.

Take time to discuss the music and lyrics with Paul, and use this as an opportunity to state family values. If Paul is unwilling to discuss them with you, clearly state what you feel is appropriate and what is allowed in the house. (Refer to Commandment 7, "Set limits. No is a complete sentence.") Paul may not like it, but at least he will be exposed by you to powerfully positive values to help combat all the negatives elsewhere.

Once the rule is explicit regarding what music is allowed in the house, let Paul know that any inappropriate tapes, etc. will be confiscated and thrown out. Let him know that his willingness to respond appropriately to rules with which he disagrees will determine the level of personal freedom he enjoys outside the home. Privileges are based on responsible behavior and responsibility includes following parental rules.

Question 13

My daughter, Debbie, has always enjoyed being a member of her church youth group, but since she turned 14, she no longer wants to go and says that all the kids there are nerds. This is a very positive group of kids, but we have been told we should not push our religious values on our daughter, that we should let her make this choice. How about it?

Answer

When children enter their teens, they become extremely involved with their image and they may classify other people in ways that make them feel superior. This classification process is a good example of the "all or none" adolescent thinking disorder. Debbie also may be wanting to avoid the church group for some other reason such as fear of rejection, guilt associated with changing values, an upsetting experience or merely a need to be involved in groups of her own choosing, not yours.

Other parenting books may say that you should not attempt to impose your values and your choice of peer groups on Debbie because she is able to do this on her own. This type of thinking supports the miniature adult theory. Realistically, it is quite likely that Debbie is incapable of doing this. She is more focused upon avoiding anxiety and improving her image than on becoming involved in positive group activity.

Initially, you might ask her what's behind her disinterest in the group and use this discussion to reassure and show understanding. However, consistent with the commandment, "Build positive values at an early age," we encourage you to insist that Debbie continue to be involved in the church youth group until you are convinced she is capable of responsibly choosing peer groups and organizations on her own. Refuse to argue when you inform her of this decision, and simply insist that, whereas she may not understand the decision at this particular time, you believe this is in her best interests. You can go on to explain that you are much more concernd about doing things that are best for her than with giving her what she wants. Continue to emphasize that if attending this particular group is not a positive experience, this is her problem and lack of responsibility, not yours. You might also add that in another year, when she is more mature and her choices have offered you more opportunity to observe her judgment, you may reconsider the matter.

Question 14

Our 13-year-old son Chuck has become disrespectful. He constantly talks back, argues and challenges limits, especially with his mother. I know that some of this is normal, but I would not have dared act this way with my parents and his behavior does not seem right to me. What can I do?

Answer

A certain amount of disrespect, rebellion and testing of parents *is* normal at this age. The purpose of this type of behavior is for adolescents to prove to themselves and their parents that they are different and therefore separate from their parents. However, although this behavior has a sound developmental rationale, it is also true that society has become increasingly tolerant of this type of negative and disrespectful behavior from kids. Parents have also learned from various self-help books that this type of behavior is normal so they resign themselves to many years of verbal abuse, thinking they have no right to take a stand. This type of thinking supports the "it's just a phase" myth.

We believe that while it is normal for adolescents to rebel, we strongly believe that parents do not have to tolerate excessive amounts of verbal abuse. Let Chuck know that although you realize he has a mind of his own, you will not tolerate abusive, disrespectful behavior from him and that this type of behavior will have consequences every time it occurs.

The best consequence for this type of behavior is a time-out, requiring Chuck to spend 15 minutes alone in his room without any other type of stimulation such as radio or TV. During this time he needs to reflect upon his feelings and gain control of them. This 15-minute time-out not only allows Chuck an opportunity to gain control, but also allows parents an opportunity to gain control of their own anger, frustration and need to be in power. Furthermore, the time-out system can be set up in such a way that if Chuck accumulates more than a certain number of time-outs in a one-week period, they are exchanged for removal of other privileges. Chuck will very quickly get the message that you will not tolerate his disrespectful behavior, and he will realize that he will need to find other ways to express his need for separation. Learning will also be accelerated if Chuck is required to process each time-out in writing (see Appendix G).

Many parents have the mistaken notion that they are obligated to fully discuss conflictual issues and limits with their children. Too many times these discussions become nothing more than an opportunity for adolescent arguing, manipulating and disrespect. When parents give reasons, teenagers often use this as an additional opportunity to challenge parental positions. It is during these "discussions" that adolescents often assert, "That's not fair." Unfortunately, fairness for adolescents tends to correspond more with what they want than to some abstract concept of justice. (Have you ever known adolescents to complain about fairness when it meant getting their own way?)

Another common parental error is the tendency to listen to all of an adolescent's reasons for wanting a particular thing or privilege. When parents listen to "I think I should get to stay out later because . . ." they simply validate and support the negotiation and argument process, as if the child were a miniature adult. If the issue is not up for negotiation, why allow arguments?

Also relevant here is the 30-second rule described in Commandment 9. In some cases, a short explanation may help Chuck understand and accept some of your limits. However, if he continues to argue or "reason," you can assume that he is either too immature or too unwilling to understand your reasons for the rule and discussion can end.

Question 15

My 14-year-old daughter Amy is obsessed with her 19-year-old boyfriend. She will sneak, lie and do almost anything to be with him. Her grades and attitude have worsened since she began to see him. What should I do?

Answer

This particular problem accounts for a large number of referrals to inpatient and outpatient treatment. The relationship between a younger female adolescent and a much older male is, in our opinion, a form of child abuse. As you have already observed, an older, more mature boy (man) is in a position to exert a tremendous amount of power over your daughter's attitude, behavior and self-esteem. In most states, a sexual relationship between a 14-year-old female and a 19-year-old male constitutes sexual abuse or statutory rape.

Amy probably sees this boy as strong, powerful and grown up, which makes her feel more like an adult. In maintaining this relationship, Amy not only increases her self-esteem in a negative way, she also validates her femininity and sexuality. Similarly, this relationship helps her feel special and important, a feeling state all teenagers strive for. Finally, this relationship gives Amy an opportunity to rebel against parental values and authority. This aspect of the relationship is likely to make her even more determined to hold on to him.

Amy is motivated by these overwhelming feelings, which often seem to resemble an addiction. The fact that her attitudes, grades and morals have suffered from this relationship is further evidence of her "addiction" to this "mood-altering" male. It is your responsibility as a parent to take a very strong stand and insist that she end this relationship. We believe this situation is very similar to the issues discussed in Commandment 10 because such relationships can be every bit as destructive to Amy and your family as sex, drugs and rock and roll.

Obviously, since Amy is overwhelmed with adolescent feelings and cannot see the destructive nature of this relationship, she will vehemently oppose your intervention and make everybody's life very difficult. Refuse to compromise and let Amy know that if she continues the relationship, she will be severely restricted both at home and in her other social relationships. Remember, Amy is not thinking clearly or she would not have become involved in the relationship to begin with, so do not expect reasoning or guilt trips to change her attitude.

After taking a stand, it is important to monitor her compliance closely. If she continues to sneak around, if she becomes severely depressed over ending the relationship, or if she becomes abusive and destructive toward you, then you need to consider getting outside help.

7

A Final Statement

Throughout this book, we have made repeated references to the process whereby our complex society interacts with an immature, evolving individual who is struggling for a sense of freedom and self-worth. Unfortunately, this interaction can be destructive, producing strong feelings of frustration and hopelessness within many families. We do not share the sense of dread experienced by many families struggling with adolescent issues, nor do we share the hopelessness generated by the media when referring to the process of growing up.

We have felt that much of the difficulty encountered by parents in dealing with adolescents stems from faulty assumptions and myths about children and parenting that have flourished particularly since the early '60s. Using an adult yardstick to evaluate teenage behavior and problems is unfair to them and leads to unnecessary frustration for parents. We hope we have convinced you that adolescents are not miniature adults — that adolescence is a stage of childhood.

With an appropriate understanding of the nature of the beast — adolescents — the impact of our chaotic society is much more easily understood. Adolescents' need for structure and guidance from parents willing to provide their time as well as their love is critical in today's world of rapid change and hedonistic values.

Raising children is a tremendous responsibility and a wonderful opportunity to affirm the value of each individual by guiding developing children to responsible maturity and healthy self-esteem. There are no short-cuts, no quick fixes and no easy answers in responsible parenting. Parents cannot give their children maturity; they have to help their children work for it themselves. This is what it means to be a parent. An old Chinese proverb quoted earlier states, "You can give a man a fish and feed him for a day, or teach him to fish and feed him for a lifetime." Parenting means helping children learn to take care of themselves.

Parenting is an important task. However, society tends to take for granted the skills required to be an effective parent. What is missing from parenting approaches over the past 25 years is a philosophy that provides the foundation for building the internal person. Using the principles described in this book, we have facilitated the growth of hundreds of families who experienced chaos and hopelessness and were able to find a workable order and mutual caring. This has resulted in our feeling much pride and hope for the future. With the publication of this book, we are committed to bringing renewed hope and happiness to families, and to making the adolescent years enjoyable and rewarding to parents, as well as to their children.

Appendix A

The Leite-Parrish Glossary Of
Adolescent Terms And Behaviors

The language used by adolescents represents and reflects their thoughts, feelings and behavior. Words reflect the view of the world that an individual holds as meaningful. Not only does the choice of a particular word or phrase describe a situation for an adolescent, it also tends to reinforce that particular view of the world through repetition and familiarity. An ability to understand and use the following terms and phrases will be extremely helpful in dealing with your adolescent.

Acceptance: The willingness on the part of adolescents to comply with social and parental limits, whether they agree with them or not.

Acting out: The expression of feeling in behavior, usually aggressive, manipulative, attention-seeking and/or destructive behavior.

Addictive: Behavior characterized by extremes, dependence, powerlessness and loss of control.

Adolerican: Alien adolescent American.

Adolescence: A developmental stage reflecting incomplete emotional, psychological, biological, perceptual and intellectual maturity. Adolescents are children, not miniature adults.

Adulthood: Developmental stage following adolescence characterized by independence, responsibility, well-defined values and maturity.

Alcohol: The most dangerous and most popular *drug* used by adolescents.

Alien: Parental description of typical adolescent behavior.

Arguing: Statements made by an adolescent in an attempt to defy a rule, push a limit, avoid a consequence or merely gain power in a verbal interaction with an authority figure. Arguments are often disguised by adolescents as discussions of what is "fair" or "right."

Attention-Seeking: Behavior aimed primarily at getting the immediate attention of others, which is frequently disruptive and self-destructive.

Attitude: Perceptions about self, others or the world that determine feelings and thinking. Can be positive or negative.

Authority: Person or institution responsible for setting limits and establishing consequences for rule violations. Authority figures serve as one form of a Higher Power for adolescents.

Bait And Switch: A manipulative technique in which adolescents avoid issues under discussion by switching to another issue with which they are more comfortable.

Behavioral Contract: A written agreement between parents and adolescents that specifies parental expectations, rules for acceptable behavior, consequences for rule violations and privileges.

Blaming: Usually a manipulative effort aimed at avoiding responsibility for one's own behavior (see Bait And Switch).

Choice: Freedom to select a course of behavior through decision-making. However, adolescents must learn to accept the consequences, positive or negative, of that choice (see Freedom, Consequences).

Commitment: As opposed to a promise, a commitment is a statement of change made to one's self that requires no audience but can be observed by others in consistent behavior.

Confused (I'm): Frequently used as an excuse for a lack of willingness and effort.

Consequence: Any problem, punishment, feeling or situation that follows or results from a particular choice of behavior. Behavior always has consequences (see Choice, Freedom).

Control: Fantasy state in which parents erroneously assume that they direct their adolescent's choices and behaviors.

Defense Mechanisms: Unconscious psychological processes that distort individual perception of events to feelings of inferiority, inadequacy, guilt or emotional pain.

Denial: Unconscious process in which reality is ignored or avoided in an attempt to reduce emotional discomfort (See Defense Mechanisms).

Dependent: Adolescent involved in the usually destructive process in which what is best is given up in pursuit of desires that are perceived as necessary for emotional or physical survival. For example, girls who are male-dependent and boys who are female-dependent.

Designated Driver: Ludicrous program based on the assumption, fostered by the media, that adolescents irresponsible enough to break the law and drink alcohol will have the good judgment to select a nondrinking person to drive.

Destructive Relationship: This refers to an interaction of two or more individuals that produces a negative result, regardless of how healthy or caring the individuals are in the relationship. If the outcome is destructive, the relationship is destructive.

Detachment: Process of achieving emotional distance and perspective in close, caring relationships.

Discipline: Feedback from the environment that informs adolescents that their approach to living, represented by their choices, is not healthy or effective.

Divergence: That part of adolescent identity formation that emphasizes differentiation.

Don't Know (I): Yet another safe response, used in place of putting forth the effort and taking the risks required to make an honest, intelligent response.

Doormat: Applies to anyone who allows others to use, dominate or walk all over them. Doormatism reflects passivity, avoidance and dishonesty.

Druggie: An individual involved in the adolescent drug culture or having an image associated with drug use.

Emotional Risking: Willingness to deal with uncomfortable situations or feelings which leads to growth.

Entitlement: Adolescent belief that parents or the world owes them something.

Equality: Mistaken belief that parents and their adolescents are equal in judgment and should have equal privileges.

Excuses: Any of a variety of statements that helps adolescents avoid accepting responsibility for their behavior.

Expectations: Parental beliefs applied to the positive, healthy development of adolescents.

External Validation: The process of using peers, material goods and image as a means of boosting self-esteem.

Facts: To the adolescent, facts refer to what is perceived, not necessarily what exists.

Feelings: Genuine emotions such as guilt, shame, hurt, anger, sadness, loneliness, fear, etc. Feelings are differentiated from thoughts.

Feelings Are Real: Refers to the fact that there is no such thing as a wrong feeling. All feelings are right. The perceptions upon which feelings are based may be inaccurate, but feelings in response to perception are always real.

Fox-Hole Promises: Insincere promises made under pressure or after being caught doing something wrong. The life span of these promises is directly related to the pressure brought to bear.

Freedom: Most adolescents feel that freedom means no restrictions. However, genuine freedom is the awareness of one's ability to choose.

Friendship Theory: Parental belief that it is more important to be a friend to an adolescent than an authority figure.

Get-Back Game: A process by which adolescents directly or indirectly attempt to hurt those who have hurt them.

Gonna (I'm): Used as a promise or statement of future intention; usually a poor substitute for effort and willingness in the present.

Guilt-Tripping: Parental attempts to produce shame or guilt in their children in an effort to mold positive behavior.

Honesty: Being open and truthful. Honesty is not a matter of degree. It is like pregnancy: either you are or you aren't.

I Can't: Usually refers to a manipulative attempt to avoid what is best. This is confronted as a self-victimizing statement and usually reflects a lack of willingness, not a lack of ability.

Identity: Stable perception of self associated with maturity.

Image: The impression that an adolescent projects to others through language, attitude and behavior including clothing, make-up and music preference.

Immaturity: Not fully formed, a characteristic of adolescence.

Individuation: Struggle to separate adolescent values and behavior from that of parents.

Institution: Publicly held social foundations that embody and impart societal values and beliefs affecting the parenting process.

Intimacy: Emotional closeness, respect and sharing, not to be confused with lust or infatuation.

Judgment: Process of making decisions, which is heavily influenced by maturity level.

KWASOMs: Kids Without Any Self-discipline Or Motivation. These kids are given everything by their parents and accomplish little on their own.

Leaking Anger: Displacing anger onto another person or inanimate object rather than dealing directly with the issue or person who is the object of the anger.

Learning Experience: Name given to a period of time out that immediately follows inappropriate behavior during which adolescents reflect on their actions. This period may precede written or verbal processing.

Lecture: Impassioned speech resembling a sermon that subscribes to the miniature adult theory when delivered to an adolescent in a misguided attempt to change behavior or discipline.

Lie: Refers to anything but the complete truth, including a lie of omission in which some important detail is left out for the purpose of misleading the listener.

Limit Testing: Normal adolescent process of challenging rules set by parents or society.

Limits: Parental structure in the form of a rule.

Listen To The Words, Trust The Behavior: Frequently flowery, impressive words are used to promise future change or mask current destructive behavior. Genuine change is reflected through consistent, positive behavior, not words alone.

Manipulation: Dishonest, indirect behavior designed to get adolescents what they want.

Materialism: Society's unhealthy preoccupation with things as a means of avoiding pain and gaining immediate gratification.

Maturity: The willingness to do what is best when what is best is different from what one wants.

Me Generation: Beginning of the legitimization of selfishness and the pursuit of pleasure at any cost.

Miniature Adult Theory: Erroneous theory which assumes that adolescents are not really children but smaller versions of their adult counterparts, and as such it is assumed that adolescents possess levels of judgment, morality and self-esteem only slightly below the adult level.

Needs: What a person has to have to survive emotionally and physically. Examples are food, shelter and emotional support. Does not include privileges, fun, stuff or other wants (see Wants).

Negative Peer: Any friend or associate who has been involved with or stands for destructive values.

Nerd: Current title associated with the lowest level of social acceptance among adolescents.

No: When stated by a parent, it is a complete sentence and requires no explanation.

Overhead: The cost of doing business. Refers to consequences or reactions of others to negative or destructive adolescent behaviors. These consequences do not change adolescent behavior but are merely accepted by adolescents as necessary to getting what they want.

Owning: Taking responsibility for a feeling, behavior or role in a given situation.

Pain: Any type of physical or emotional discomfort which can be an opportunity for growth.

Parenting: Process of guiding, not controlling, children to adulthood.

Peer Group: Other adolescents of approximately the same age through whom teenagers attempt to gain acceptance and positive socialization.

Peerus Pressuritis: Leite-Parrish term referring to the horrible disease of peer pressure.

People-Pleasing: Doing something just to get approval from others rather than because it is honest and actually in one's own best interest.

Popular: Long-standing adolescent term reflecting the highest form of adolescent social status or peer acceptance.

Premature Affluence: Adolescent tendency to focus on luxuries and wants in their spending habits that reflects a standard of living far exceeding their level of maturity and financial productivity.

Privacy: A privilege, not a right, which is earned through trustworthy behavior.

Processing: Written or verbal explanation that facilitates learning or understanding of a rule violation and appropriate consequences. Used as an adjunct to behavioral contracts.

Promise: A statement made by an adolescent designed to get any other person off the adolescent's back, or a statement made to get a parent or other significant figure to grant a desire or want.

Punishment: Personalized, often aggressive act toward a child that functions more as a means of channeling parental frustration than an attempt to influence adolescent behavior.

Quick Fix: Attempt to obtain immediate gratification through material goods, drugs, sex, etc.

Reciprocity: Mistaken assumption by parents that their concern and good intentions will be returned at the same level by their adolescents.

Risking: Doing something hard or anxiety-producing that challenges destructive methods of coping, confronts blocks to change or enhances growth-oriented behavior.

Self-Esteem: The evaluation of oneself as competent and worthwhile, a positive feeling about oneself as capable and caring that comes from doing what is best, hard, scary, etc.

Sorry: Behavior change that an adolescent undertakes in response to having become aware (either through confrontation or insight) of destructive, negative behavior on his or her part. The statement "I'm sorry" is not enough.

Stamp Collecting: Adolescents often collect and save resentments toward others, especially parents, and later "redeem" or "cash them in" with lies, aggression and acting out, while feeling no guilt because adolescents believe that they are entitled to these negative behaviors as payment or prizes owed to them by the parents who have wronged them.

Structure: Limits, rules and expectations that define the environment in which adolescent development occurs.

Stuff: Such material items as clothes, VCRs, cars, jewelry, etc. Often both parents and adolescents overemphasize the value of stuff, rather than valuing relationships, accomplishments and responsibility.

Thirty-Second Rule: Any explanation for a decision or consequence that lasts longer than 30 seconds reflects ineffective communication.

Tire Tracks: Imaginary marks on the backs of weak parents who have let their kids run all over them.

Trust: Degree to which parents assume that their adolescents are behaving in an honest, responsible manner.

Trustworthiness: Level of honesty and responsibility. Since honesty and responsibility are related directly to maturity and adolescents are not completely mature, no adolescent is 100-percent trustworthy.

Trying: The time spent deciding whether you will or whether you won't. "I am trying" is usually nothing more than an excuse for a lack of 100 percent effort in a given situation.

Two-Mistake Test: Parental process of decision-making in limit-setting that emphasizes the safer, more conservative approach.

Using Behavior: Behavior associated with drug-taking or drug-taking attitudes reflecting negative values.

Values: Basic beliefs about self, others and the world that motivate behavior regardless of the situation. Honesty, integrity, caring and responsibility are examples.

Victim: Victims allow themselves to be used by others and see themselves as not having any responsibility for or control over their behavior. Self-pity and anger usually are emotional companions to this self-perception.

Wants: Desires, usually referring to things or experiences that are pleasurable or lead to pleasure. Not to be confused with needs.

"Why Not?": Usually mistaken by an adult as a request for explanation when in fact it is merely a manipulation aimed at changing a no to a yes.

Willingness: The decision to put forth effort to accomplish a task, regardless of how hard, frustrating, scary, etc. Does not mean a successful outcome but rather 100 percent effort.

Appendix B

Sample Contract

(Your contract should reflect your child's developmental age in regard to specific limits.)

This behavioral contract, dated May 21, 1990, is between Jennifer Smith, age 14, and her parents, Bill and Mary Smith. The purpose of this contract is to give written structured guidance to Jennifer in the form of rules, limits and responsibilities to govern her behavior in and out of the home. If concerns arise that are not specifically outlined in this contract, they will be dealt with at the discretion of her parents at the point and time such concern is apparent. Any necessary modifications to this contract will be made at the next family meeting.

Areas of Opportunity	Responsibilities	Consequences for Irresponsibility/Violation
1. Peer relations	1. All friends must be introduced complete with last names and home phone numbers. Association with peers who drink alcohol, take other drugs, smoke or who project negative attitudes and images is not allowed. Association with any peer must be approved.	1. First — immediate termination with negative peer and loss of all privileges for three days. Second — immediate termination with negative peer and loss of all privileges for one week.
A. After school and weekends	A. Only with permission. Do not ask permission to go see friends or have friends over unless all homework and chores are complete.	A. First — loss of visiting privileges for one week. Second — loss of visiting privileges for two weeks.
B. Social activities, one night per weekend	B. Parents must receive three days notice. Parents must know where, with whom and a phone number to call in case of emergency. Activities must be parent-supervised. It is your responsibility to prove that you are where you say you are.	B. First — loss of weekend social activity for one week. Second — loss of weekend social activity for one month.
C. Dating	C. Only in groups and at pre-approved places with adult supervision. No secret romances.	C. Loss of weekend privileges for following weekend.

2. Curfew

2. Late is late, be it five minutes or a half hour.

A. School nights

A. 8:00 p.m. or before dark. Special circumstances will require 24 hours notice.

A. First — curfew 30 minutes earlier for one week.
Second — loss of all outside social activities for one week.

B. Weekends and holidays

B. 10:00 p.m. unless previous permission is given to extend time and only if accompanied by a mature, responsible adult.

B. Same as above.

3. School

3. Must maintain at least a C average in all subjects.

3. If a six weeks grade falls below C, begin one additional hour in study time for that subject until grade is brought up.

A. Homework

A. Homework needs to be completed daily. No phone calls, TV or radio when studying. Do not wait until the last minute to do large projects. Seek help right away for trouble in a subject; do not wait until it becomes a major problem.

A. If homework is not complete, loss of phone, stereo and TV privileges for next day.

B. Conduct

B. Satisfactory conduct in each class. No tardies.

B. First — loss of phone, stereo and radio for one week for each unsatisfactory. Loss of phone, stereo and radio for one day for each tardy.

Areas of Opportunity	Responsibilities	Consequences for Irresponsibility/Violation
4. Phone	4. Using the telephone is not a right, but a privilege. Fifteen-minute limit on all calls. Parent reserves the right to monitor any phone call that arouses suspicion. No long-distance calls without permission.	
A. School nights	A. No calls during study time. No calls after 10:00 p.m.	A. First — no calls on school nights for 2 days. Second — no calls on school nights for 1 week. Continued abuse will result in no phone calls on school nights.
B. Weekends	B. Unlimited calls within reason. No calls after 10:00 p.m.	B. First — no phone calls for one weekend. Second — no phone calls for two weekends. Repeated offenses will result in no phone call privileges on weekends.
5. Bedtime	5. Sleep and rest are necessary for health, growth, and well-being. Bedtimes reflect those needs.	
A. School nights	A. 10:00 p.m. bedtime unless special circumstances are designated by parents.	A. Bedtime next night is earlier dependent on length of time late to bed.

B. Weekends

B. 12:00 p.m. bedtime

B. Bedtime next weekend night is earlier dependent on the length of time late to bed.

C. Wake-up

C. You must wake yourself up and be fully ready to leave for school at 7:45 a.m. No nagging or reminding from parents.

C. Loss of phone privileges for the day or an earlier bedtime that night.

6. Household chores

6. Everyone living in the house has a responsibility to contribute to the upkeep of the house.

A. Room

A. Keep drawers, closet and bath neat and tidy. Make sure dirty clothes are put in hamper immediately after removing. Keep vanity neat and orderly. Do not let laundry pile up.

A. Loss of phone, stereo and outside privileges until room is clean.

B. Dishes

B. Rinse off own dishes and put in dishwasher before leaving the kitchen after evening meals.

B. First — do all dishes the next two days. Second — do all dishes and clean bathroom for next two days.

Areas of Opportunity	Responsibilities	Consequences for Irresponsibility/Violation
C. Miscellaneous	C. If you turn it on, turn it off. If you move it, put it back. If you borrow it, return it. If you make a mess, clean it up. If you open it, close it. If you break it, fix it. If you can't fix it, report it. If it doesn't concern you, don't mess with it. If you don't know, ask.	C. To be determined depending on the area of irresponsibility.
7. Personal	7. It is each individual's responsibility to practice good personal hygiene.	
A. Clothing, Make-up	A. Neat dress, light make-up, good judgment in jewelry and hairstyles.	A. Loss of free choice and subject to control and daily inspection by parents.
B. Borrowing	B. Do not borrow or lend clothing, jewelry or other personal belongings without permission.	B. First — loss of phone for three days. Second — loss of all weekend privileges.
C. Church/Synagogue	C. Attend one church/synagogue function of your choice per week.	C. Loss of one weekend privilege, to be determined by parents.

D. Allowance

D. $10 per week to be used for outside activities, gifts and wants.

D. Irresponsible use or spending on anything illegal will result in loss or reduction of allowance.

8. Conduct/Relationships

8. Household harmony is important to everyone. It is important that harmony be maintained.

A. Basic respect

A. No arguing, disrespect, cursing, manipulation or tantrums.

A. 15 minutes of timeout (LE) in room with no radio, stereo or phone, to reflect upon the problem (per offense) and completion of processing form. More than four LEs per week results in additional loss of privileges.

B. First — 3 day restriction of all privileges.
   Second — 1 week restriction of all privileges.
   Third — to be discussed.

C. To be discussed.

B. Honesty

B. No lying.

C. Drugs and alcohol

C. Absolutely no use of alcohol or other drugs, including cigarettes.

9. Electronic media

9. Statement of overall viewing and listening policy.

A. TV

A. Watch only shows approved by parents. One hour per day only on music video channel. No R-rated movies.

A. First — restriction of TV privileges for three days.
   Second — restriction of TV privileges for one week.

Areas of Opportunity	Responsibilities	Consequences for Irresponsibility/Violation
B. Radio	B. Listen only to channels approved by parents. No listening while doing homework.	B. First — loss of radio for three days. Second — loss of radio for one week.
C. Stereo	C. All albums, CDs, tapes and posters must be approved. No heavy metal, punk rock or filthy rap.	C. First — destroy negative tapes, etc. and loss of stereo for three days. Second — destroy negative tapes, etc. and loss of stereo for one week.

Our signatures below indicate we fully understand the terms and guidelines of this contract.

_____   _____

Appendix C

Signs Of Alcohol And Drug Use

The following is a comprehensive list of signs and symptoms associated with alcohol and other drug use. No single item (other than acute intoxication) is a certain sign of drug use. However, when any of the following items is observed, especially when several are seen together, parents need to be aware that drug use could be the underlying cause of this behavior. We include this lengthy list to sensitize parents to the possible existence of a drug problem.

Behavioral Signs While Under The Influence

1. Red eyes
2. Dilated pupils, unusual eye movements
3. Slurred speech
4. Unsteady walk
5. Unusual complexion — pale or flushed
6. Inappropriate giggling or laughter
7. Sudden appetite (munchies)
8. Alcohol on breath
9. Smelling like mouthwash, gum or mints after being with peers

10. Attention, concentration difficulty
11. Seeing or hearing things not noticed by others

Behavioral Signs Of Repetitive Use Pattern

1. Cigarette smoking
2. Change in values, attitude
3. Change in appearance, negative imagery in clothing
4. Heavy metal or punk rock T-shirts
5. Decrease in personal hygiene
6. Emotional sensitivity and overreaction to criticism
7. Change in peer group
8. Avoids bringing friends home, refers to them by first name only
9. Loss of motivation or ambition
10. Withdrawal from family
11. Spends majority of time at home in room
12. Dropping of previous interests
13. Change in eating patterns
14. Unexplained weight loss or gain
15. Increasing self-centeredness
16. Lack of concern for others
17. Demand for immediate gratification
18. Phone-call secretiveness, callers refuse to identify themselves
19. Callers hang up, odd hours calls
20. Money or items disappearing from home
21. Change in sleeping patterns
22. Accident proneness
23. Frequent or persistent illness
24. Severe oppositional behavior
25. DUI, multiple traffic violations, accidents
26. Shoplifting
27. Gets angry if parents come into room without knocking
28. Increasingly aggressive behavior

29. Preoccupation with weapons
30. Excessive interest in the occult

School-Related Behavioral Signs

1. Excessive tardiness
2. Skipping school
3. Drop in grades
4. Sleeping in class
5. Poor conduct reports/disrespect/insubordination/ arguing/profanity
6. Withdrawal from school activities
7. Reports of daydreaming
8. Unusual errors in homework or assignments
9. Decrease in ambition, discussion or future plans
10. School suspension, expulsion
11. Disrespect toward teachers

Paraphernalia

1. Rolling papers
2. Pipes
3. Incense
4. Eye drops/mouthwash/breath mints
5. Room deodorizers
6. Hemostats
7. Cocaine kit: razor blade, small straw, mirror, small spoon, vials
8. Stash cans
9. Locked boxes
10. Drug-related books, magazines
11. Heavy metal music posters, T-shirts
12. Hypodermic needles
13. Knives and guns
14. Used nitrous oxide containers
15. Whiskey bottle/beer cans
16. Empty prescription bottles
17. Old rags (used for huffing gas or other solvents)

18. Used glue/Magic Markers/Liquid Paper container
19. Empty freon or Scotchguard cans
20. Candles/remains of animals/books associated with satanic rituals

Appendix D

Warning Signs Of
Potentially Impaired Parental Judgment

Feeling extreme anger or rage toward your adolescent.

Using physical force in an attempt to gain or maintain control.

Persistent marital conflict over parenting practices.

Feeling that your kids are unmanageable.

Avoiding conflict out of fear that your adolescent will run away, commit suicide or act aggressively toward you.

Personalizing your adolescent's behavior, i.e., "He/ She behaves that way just to make me crazy."

Constantly making excuses and "bailing out" your adolescent in response to problem behaviors.

Excessive or increased use of alcohol or other drugs on your part.

Appendix E

Checklist Of Negative Peer Characteristics

Friends without limits, curfews or parental supervision

Friends who reflect a negative image in their clothing or appearance (earrings, heavy metal concert shirts, deviant haircuts)

Friends about whom your adolescent is vague or evasive regarding their identity (no last name, nicknames only, no exact address)

Friends who contact your adolescent only outside the home (meet in parking lots or hangouts, phone calls late at night, callers who hang up if a parent answers)

Friends who have a history of legal problems, school suspensions or school dropouts

Friends who are more than two years older

Appendix F

Warning List Of Serious Adolescent Depression

Dramatic change in attitude, behavior or lifestyle
Excessive moodiness, irritability or crying spells
Change in sleep and appetite
Ongoing feelings of hopelessness and despair
Vague suicidal statements ("I wish I had never been born")
Decreased effort and interest in activities formerly enjoyed
Extreme withdrawal from family or friends
A significant drop in grades
Reading and writing of poems, books, stories and movies with sad, violent or hopeless themes.

Appendix G

Sample Learning Experience
Processing Form

Sample ideal answers appear in italics after each question.

1. What did I do or not do to earn the time-out? *(Argued with Mom.)*
2. What behavior do I need to change to avoid this problem in the future? *(Don't talk back.)*
3. What attitude change is necessary to correct this behavior? *(Realize that no is a complete sentence and that I can't always get my way.)*
4. What would the consequences be for this type of behavior outside the family or in the adult world? *(Teacher would give me detention, I could get fired from a job.)*
5. What have I learned from this experience? *(Arguing causes more problems.)*

References

Andre, Pierre. **Drug Addiction. Learn About It Before Your Kids Do.** Pompano Beach, FL: Health Communications, Inc., 1988.

Ellis, Dan. **Growing Up Stoned.** Pompano Beach, FL: Health Communications, Inc., 1986.

Erikson, Erik. **Identity: Youth and Crisis.** New York, NY: W.W. Norton and Company, 1968.

Freud, S.A. "Three Essays on the Theory of Sexuality." *Standard Edition*, Vol. VII. London: The Hogarth Press, 1953.

O'Gorman, Patricia and Philip Oliver-Diaz. **Breaking The Cycle Of Addiction.** Pompano Beach, FL: Health Communications, Inc., 1987.

Piaget, J. **The Moral Judgment of the Child.** London: Routledge and Kegan Paul, 1932 or, see: Glencoe, IL: The Free Press, 1948.

Rice, P.E. **The Adolescent: Development, Relationships, and Culture,** 2nd Ed. Boston, MA: Allyn and Bacon, Inc., 1978.